A Rocky Mountain Christmas

second edition

A ROCKY MOUNTAIN CHRISTMAS

Yuletide Stories of the West

JOHN H. MONNETT

PRUETT PUBLISHING COMPANY
BOULDER, COLORADO

Cover and book design by Jody Chapel, Cover to Cover Design, Denver, Colorado
Cover painting by Jon Crane

Printed in the United States

10 9 8 7 6 5 4 3 2

Library of Congress Cataloging-in-Publication Data

Monnett, John H.
    A Rocky Mountain Christmas: Yuletide stories of the West / John
  H. Monnett.
        p.   cm.
    Includes bibliographical references and index.
    ISBN 0-87108-830-4 (alk. paper)
    1. Christmas—West (U.S.)—History. I. Title.
GT4986.W47M66   1992
394.2'68282'0978—dc20   92-16281
                                                              CIP

This book is dedicated to the memory of the western artist C. M. Russell, whose original Christmas cards sent to members of my family during the early years of this century inspired the words on these pages.

Contents

Preface

This is a new edition of *A Rocky Mountain Christmas: Yuletide Stories of the West,* first published in 1987. A number of errors in the first edition have been corrected, and two new pioneer reminiscences have been included. "Good Neighbors" first appeared in *Western Horseman,* December 1991. It is the story of how a few farmers and ranchers put aside their differences and cooperated for their mutual survival during a severe blizzard that hit the Great Plains in December 1880. The other new chapter, "Snowbound," is from the reminiscences of a circuit-riding clergyman who became stranded on the Kansas prairie during the Christmas of 1855.

Indeed, the theme of hardship in the face of the elements seems to be a common thread that binds many pioneers' Christmas memories. With the success of the first edition of *A Rocky Mountain Christmas* have come many tales of Christmases past told to me by interested readers wishing to relate favorite holiday tales about a member of their family a generation or two removed or even the story of a distant ancestor. Each saga has some element of adversity as well as the means by which the participant overcame the obstacle and celebrated Christmas anyway.

Considering this shared motif of hardship, which more often than not characterizes holiday memories, one (especially a writer) must speculate about the "degree" of authenticity of many of these tales. As a professional historian, I have often cringed over the number of years, even decades, that separate some of these events from their initial telling. Indeed, if our ancestors' memories are anything like mine and yours, they probably remembered past events in a somewhat time-filtered fashion, especially if the memories were from childhood. Was Kit Carson's engagement party really the gala soiree that trapper O. P. Wiggins remembered? Wiggins idolized Carson and was known to frequently "embellish the truth." Were Reverend Cyrus Townsend Brady's encounters with homesteaders really as evocative as he remembered? Brady wrote in the romantic allegorical tradition of the late nineteenth century.

Possibly the answer may be found in the striking similarities of the remembrances of nineteenth-century Americans and those of twentieth-century Americans. The element of "keeping the holiday" despite adversity is universal and timeless and as such links us to our pioneer past. Modern Americans, too, remember their Christmases past as larger-than-life events.

With the prolonged interest today in revisionist interpretations of Western history, often focusing on the negative results of pioneering for present generations and the failure of most frontiersmen to fulfill the dreams they sought in the West, it is interesting to note that many pioneers still remembered Christmas much as you and I do. Even from the perspective of popular history, we can learn almost as much from *how* our ancestors remembered the holidays as we can from *what* they remembered. The reminiscences of pioneers in the Rocky Mountain West reaffirm the original lure of the frontier—not the promise of great material accomplishment but rather the hope for a new chance, and possibly, spiritual betterment. After all, isn't that what Christmas is really all about?

Acknowledgments

I wish to express my sincere gratitude to the staffs of the state historical societies of Colorado, Montana, New Mexico, and Wyoming, who provided information for this volume. Special thanks go to the staff of the Western History Department of the Denver Public Library. The staff's assistance and the Library's archives were paramount to the completion of this project. I am especially thankful for the caring patience in putting up with my fumbling hours at the microfilm readers.

To the staff members of Norlin Library at the University of Colorado, Boulder; the Auraria Library in Denver, Colorado; and the Boulder Public Library—I am in your debt.

Thanks also is extended to my past students at Metropolitan State College who put me onto some very fine material. Finally, I am eternally indebted to my wife, Linda, "Editor in Chief," who spent hours reading and correcting the manuscript during all stages of its development.

Introduction

During the doleful autumn of 1859, a solitary gold prospector by the name of William Barney completed the crude but roomy log cabin that would insure his survival through the long winter ahead. The cabin was situated near a bubbling mountain stream that spilled out onto the dusty plains from a picturesque shaded canyon. Barney had felled virgin timber from the banks of the silvery little stream to construct a rough-hewn plank wood floor and the outer walls of his dwelling. The spaces between the logs were chinked with mud, and tanned hides were fastened to the open window to bring in light while keeping out the fierce winds. Stores of wild game were salted and laid in for the long winter.

On December 25 a Christmas dance was held at Barney's cabin because it had the only wooden floor in the primitive settlement. Two hundred men and seventeen women attended the festivities. A late dinner was prepared in the open air; it consisted of venison, rabbit, and cutthroat trout caught in the nearby stream. Coffee was served from steel wash boilers that had rattled across the plains in a Murphy wagon. Many of the guests dressed in flour sacks and borrowed shirts, and it is simply recorded that everyone had an enjoyable time.

Thus passed the first documented Christmas celebration held in Boulder, Colorado (then part of the Nebraska Territory) at what is today the corner of Eleventh and Pearl Streets. The simple festivity was typical of many early Yuletide observances held in scores of "instant communities" that sprang up in the wilds of the Rocky Mountains during the middle years of the nineteenth century. It was typical in the sense that early pioneers on the western frontier could plant civilization and culture in the savage new land only by adapting older practices within the parameters of available natural resources. Bringing with them what they could from their established homes far away, these ambitious adventurers blended elements of the old with the resources of the new frontier. In doing so, they changed society and built a nation.

When in 1893 historian Frederick Jackson Turner presented his landmark treatise *The Significance of the Frontier in American History* at the Chicago World's Fair, he laid the foundation for explaining the development of American culture through the process of necessary adaptation and modification along the successive frontiers of this nation. Turner said:

> The peculiarity of American institutions is the fact that they have been compelled to adapt themselves to the changes of an expanding people — to the changes involved in crossing a continent, in winning a wilderness, and developing at each area of this progress out of the primitive economic and political conditions of the frontier into the complexity of city life. . . . The true point of view in the history of this nation is not the Atlantic coast, it is the Great West.

Due to the raw nature of the wilderness environment devoid of the luxuries of civilization, pioneers were forced to change their ways of doing things. Innovation and adaptation in politics, economics, and social life characterized those who survived. And so it was with their celebrations of Christmas.

Christmas was the one time in the long year the pioneer would take for needed respite, reflection upon the previous year, and formulation of hopes and dreams for the future. Whether snowbound as a member of a military exploring expedition caught in an uncharted mountain pass or dancing at midnight like William Barney in a crude gold rush cabin, the pioneer tried to observe the Yuletide. Of course, most of the elaborate trappings of Christmas that western settlers had known back East did not exist on the great void of the American frontier. Taking from nature what they could find, early pioneers made the best Christmas they could until civilization caught up with them. Where evergreen was unavailable, other natural vegetation was substituted. Gifts and ornaments were lovingly fashioned from the land, and feasts of wild game replaced Christmas dinners formerly obtained from a city poulterer.

The pioneer brought about modifications of Christmas customs in social practice as well. Prowess in hunting was a necessity in the new communities, and pioneers transformed their Yuletide celebrations into competitive sporting events to test marksmanship skills. Community festivities electric with optimism for the future characterized many early celebrations in the West. Perhaps the most drastic example of modified Yuletide practices occurred among the Native American inhabitants of the West who integrated elements of the white man's Christianity into their ancient religions at Christmastime.

In the following pages I have tried to illustrate the sometimes novel, sometimes sentimental, and sometimes austere adaptations our pioneer ancestors in the Rocky Mountain West incorporated into their celebrations of Christmas. From the first days of exploration, through the colorful era of the boisterous mountain men, and into the bustling gold and silver camps, isolated ranches, and homestead farms, the pageant of Christmas was played out over the generations, among soldiers on the frontier, in the cities, and in the remote Indian camps and pueblos.

I have tried to include most geographical regions within and adjacent to the Rocky Mountains, ranging from the Canadian border in the north to New Mexico in the south. The book is not limited to the mountains themselves. The development of the Great Basin by the Mormon pioneers of Utah and the tremendous wave of pioneer farmers and cattlemen who engulfed the Great Plains to the east of the Continental Divide all played decisive roles in the evolution of the Rocky Mountain states and are therefore included in these pages.

Some of the stories and accounts were extracted from relatively obscure sources and are being told here for the first time since the nineteenth century. Others are quite well known and are included for their color and significance to the development of Christmas customs in the Rocky Mountain West. Undoubtedly, there are many stories yet to be discovered, and this work is by no means exhaustive. It is my sincere hope that you enjoy the stories for what they are—a nostalgic look through the window of time to view simple Christmas dramas and the pleasures and tribulations that were near to the hearts of our pioneer ancestors.

Part One

THE
EARLY YEARS

· One ·

Christmas Comes to the Rocky Mountains 1804–1848

The American celebration of Christmas came to the Rocky Mountain West on December 25, 1804. There was no fanfare—no religious service, no decorated evergreen, no brightly wrapped gifts. In fact, that first recorded celebration went virtually unnoticed, unheralded by anyone. Only thirty-two participants attended. They had no choice—they were isolated hundreds of wilderness miles from hearth and home, and all of them would have preferred to be somewhere else. They had constructed a cottonwood log fortification in which the celebration was held. It provided some conviviality, but mostly it provided protection from the raw and dangerous land around them.

Only one year before, the very soil on which they trod had not even belonged to them. With the Louisiana Purchase in 1803, the infant nation known as the United States doubled in size with the stroke of a pen. The price was fifteen cents an acre. The western border of the new nation had once ended at the sorrel Mississippi River, but the gleaming *cordillera* of the Rocky Mountains now marked the limit of the nation—imperious France had relinquished her claims in the New World.

Early in 1803, the bold and provocative young president, Thomas Jefferson, ordered a grand expedition to the faraway mountains to explore the natural resources of the region and, he hoped, discover a navigable watercourse across the continent to the great western ocean. In command of the little party of explorers were a twenty-eight-year-old frontiersman from the Blue Ridge Mountains by the name of Meriwether Lewis and thirty-two-year-old William Clark, younger brother of the renowned George Rogers Clark. The expedition left St. Louis in the spring of 1804, ascending the Missouri River in iron-reinforced keelboats. With the first blasts of autumn, they halted and constructed a crude blockhouse that they named Fort Mandan for the Indians who lived in the vicinity.

Christmas 1804 found the expedition members shivering in this rustic outpost deep in the Dakota wilderness. (They would remain there all winter before plunging into the rugged northern Rockies in what is today central Montana.) To say the least, every member of the party missed loved ones back in the States. On Christmas morning a few volleys from small arms were fired to hail the holiday—that did little to cheer the men. Otherwise, this Christmas Day seemed like any other day in the confines of the small stockade.

Eventually, however, extra rations of brandy were ordered and a mild celebration was inaugurated. Soon the men in the party began singing songs of home. Music emanated from a violin—then a bugle, a tambourine, a mouth organ. Later in the day, a feast of buffalo meat and venison was enjoyed by all. As the brandy took effect, songs became more raucous, and men danced "merry jigs" into the night. The drinking continued until 9:00 P.M.; it enabled the men to forget their loneliness. The written record of the occasion, the first documented Christmas celebration in the Rocky Mountain West, consists of two paragraphs in a weathered log book. It was an anticlimax in the middle of a bold adventure story, but the American ritual of Christmas had come to the West, and it would endure in the future.

The simple observation of Christmas recorded in the journals of Lewis and Clark was typical of Yuletide celebrations (if they existed at all) among the first explorers who entered the boundless wilds of the Rocky Mountains. Devoid of white settlements or even overland transportation arteries connecting the wilderness with civilization, the region contained nothing that was familiar to these rugged explorers. At Christmastime they thought of home and family. In most cases, extra rations of whiskey or brandy was the only thing that helped them forget their isolation.

The Louisiana country was a big land, mostly unexplored and fraught with danger. In some instances, explorers found themselves in miserable or even life-threatening situations, where a Christmas fest like the one held at Fort Mandan would seem a civilized luxury. While Lewis and Clark were making their triumphant journey home, other expeditions were being sent into the southern reaches of the new land. The most important of these departed Belle Fontaine near St. Louis, Missouri on July 15, 1806. The little party of twenty-four soldiers was under the command of Lieutenant Zebulon Montgomery Pike. A primary objective of their trek was to "ascertain the direction, extent, and navigation of the Arkansas and Red Rivers."

The party crossed what is today the state of Kansas, following the Arkansas River across the great buffalo plains. On November 16 Pike first viewed the Rocky Mountains, including the massive peak that today bears his name. Turning south along the foothills, the little group of soldiers was hit by a fierce snowstorm near the vicinity of present-day Pueblo, Colorado. On December 1 Pike wrote, "The storm still continuing with violence, we remaind [sic]; the snow by night one foot deep; our horses being obliged to scrape it away, to obtain their miserable pittance."

By December 24 the command reached the site of present-day Salida, Colorado. The snow was deep and game had been scarce. It had not been unusual for the men to go without food for two or three days at a time. Starvation was a real possibility. Happily, the hunting party that was sent out that morning returned to camp with the joyous news that eight buffalo had been shot. Pike commented in his journal:

> We now again found ourselves all assembled together on Christmas Eve, and appeared generally to be content, although all the refreshment we had to celebrate the holiday with was buffalo meat, without salt, or any other thing whatever.

Christmas Day, Pike recorded, was stormy and bitter cold. There was no occasion for celebration. The men sat huddled around their fires reflecting upon past Christmases spent at home with their families. Zebulon Montgomery Pike recorded his own thoughts and feelings on that gray, somber Christmas afternoon:

> Here I must take the liberty of observing that in this situation, the hardships and privations we underwent, were on this day brought more fully to our mind. Having been accustomed in the past to some degree of relaxation; but here 800 miles from the frontiers of our country, in the most inclement season of the year; not one person clothed for the winter, many without blankets [having cut them up for socks, etc.] and now laying down at night on the snow or wet ground; one side burning whilst the other was pierced with the cold wind; this was in part the situation of the party whilst some were endeavoring to make a miserable substitute of raw buffalo hide for shoes. I will not speak of diet, as I conceive that to be benieth [sic] the serious consideration of a man on a voyage of such nature. We spent the day as agreeably as could be expected from men in our situation.

Forty-two years after that first Christmas spent by Americans in what is today the state of Colorado, Colonel John C. Fremont made his fourth exploring expedition to the far West. Christmas 1848 found his party camped high in the La Garita Range of southern Colorado. The experienced frontiersmen in Fremont's command named the wretched little log outpost they constructed Camp Desolation. Game had migrated into lower ranges, so that meat was not plentiful. Snow and cold had kept the hunting parties in camp close to the fires. Cold and miserable, the men in the beleaguered command were nevertheless determined to celebrate the holiday. Thomas E. Breckenridge, a member of the expedition, recorded the whimsical menu of the improvised Christmas feast:

BILL OF FARE
CAMP DESOLATION
DECEMBER 25, 1848

Soup
Mule Tail

Meats
Mule Steak, Fried Mule, Mule Chops, Boiled Mule, Stewed Mule, Boiled Mule, Scrambled Mule, Shirred Mule, French-Fried Mule, Minced Mule, Damned Mule, Mule on Toast (without the toast), Short Ribs of Mule with Apple Sauce (without the apple sauce)

Beverages
Snow, Snow Water, Water

Breckenridge concluded that, "It really makes no difference how our meat was cooked. It was the same old mule."

Despite the romance and glory that history has ascribed to the hardships experienced by the first U.S. explorers in the Rocky Mountain West, in reality these explorers were like any soldiers who have spent months or years away from home, stationed on some far-flung frontier of the world. At Christmastime melancholy deeply pervaded their thoughts and emotions. Because they were not intent upon settling permanently in the new land, they left very little of cultural significance. They established no ritual Christmas traditions in the wilderness they explored. Yet over the trails they blazed and through the great mountain passes they discovered were to come thousands of pioneers, who would conquer the West. The founders of towns and cities throughout the Rocky Mountain empire could not have succeeded if it were not for the efforts of these early government explorers—they opened the gates of civilization. And through the magnificent portals that are the Rocky Mountains, there would pass a host of trappers, traders, miners, and town builders. Herdsmen and farmers would settle the grassy flanks of the regal peaks, and they would bring with them rich cultural traditions from every corner of the young nation and from exotic foreign lands. Soon the lusty pioneers would break down the forbidden barriers of the old Spanish empire in the

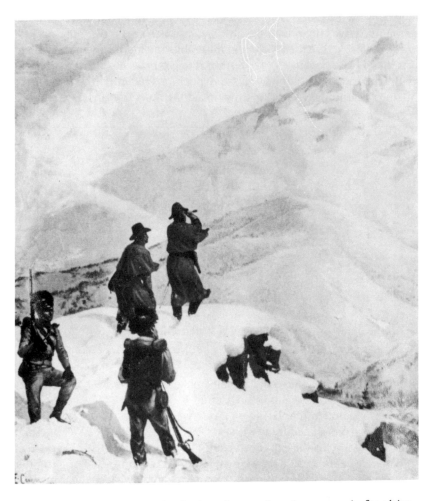

Zebulon Montgomery Pike facing the peak to be named after him.
—Denver Public Library, Western History Department

Southwest, absorbing the profuse and luxuriant traditions of Spain and Mexico in the process. Epochal customs of Christmas took root, mixing and adapting in a multicultural backdrop and rising from bold forests, mountain peaks, and prairie wilderness that gave character to the country and the men and women who settled there. Within the span of a century, the Rocky Mountains would boast some of the most colorful celebrations of Yuletide to be found anywhere in the world.

The mountain men were the
unofficial explorers of the
Rocky Mountains.

Denver Public Library,

Western History Department

· Two ·

The Mountain Men
Celebrate Christmas
1813–1855

uring the years following the Louisiana Purchase, hundreds of trappers came to the Rocky Mountain West, inspired by the booming markets for fashionable furs in the East and in Europe. From the precipitous Canadian Rockies to the mysterious Sangre de Cristos in northern Mexico, these enterprising eccentrics spread out through the wilderness, setting their trap lines in the path of the industrious beaver. The realization that Native American populations could be employed cheaply to trap even more animals and the promise that peltry was more prolific "over in the next valley," led the mountain men to probe almost every creek and stream in the mountain West. These unofficial explorers of the Rocky Mountains discovered passes through great peaks and fertile interior valleys previously unseen by government explorers.

The mountain men were the first substantial group of frontiersmen to establish semipermanent residence in the Rocky Mountain region. As they combined social practices from the East with the rich culture and ritual of the American Indian, they developed a most colorful society. This color extended to their clamorous (as sometimes caricatured) celebrations of Christmas.

During the initial years of the trade, the great fur companies constructed a series of private forts in the high river valleys. At Christmastime these deep wilderness stockades, which served as winter quarters for many trappers, became the scenes of boisterous Christmas celebrations. Drinking, feasting, and sporting contests made up most of the activities. Religious services were rarely held. With the notable exception of the Bible-quoting Jedediah Smith, most of the old mountain men's religious beliefs became more compatible with the Indian concept of harmony with nature rather than a fundamentalist form of Christianity. In fact, many of the early Christmas celebrations held in the mountains included liberal numbers of Native American participants.

Perhaps the earliest Christmas to be celebrated by the mountain men took place in the pine-clad hills and broad meadows that flank the mouth of the Missoula River in what is today northwestern Montana. There, near the base of the rugged Bitterroot Mountains, a group of Astorians constructed a crude outpost they named Fort McMillan. On Christmas Day in 1813, wintering trappers from the fort brought in a number of mountain sheep for a great Yuletide feast. Liberal supplies of tobacco and fifteen gallons of prime rum were distributed from the fort's private stores for the occasion.

The jocularity of the day was temporarily dampened by the sudden appearance of a large war party of Flathead Indians, whose recent excursion to the buffalo ranges on the eastern plains had yielded a number of Blackfoot captives. After much heated argument, the Astorians persuaded the Flatheads to release the captive Blackfoot women and children in the spirit of the white man's "holiday of giving." In return the trappers promised to provide the Flatheads with guns and ammunition to defend their villages from Blackfoot raids during the new year. The warriors were then invited to the feast, where they participated in marksmanship contests during the afternoon outside the walls of the fort.

As the fur trade spread throughout the Rockies, great feasts of wild game became characteristic of the trapper's Christmas celebration. Among the Indian tribes frequenting the trading forts, the day became known throughout the region as "The Big Eating." For one Yuletide festival at Fort Union, Montana, James Kipp, a grizzled veteran of the fur trade, planned to give his trappers and their Indian allies a real "Eastern" delicacy for Christmas dinner. During the weeks before Christmas, Kipp fattened a large heifer, a rare commodity at that time in the mountains. He reasoned the meat would provide a Christmas surprise for his men.

Kipp, however, was the one taken by surprise. After eating only a small portion of the beef, the diners fell silent and shortly, throwing all pretense of propriety aside, adamantly refused the meat. Returning to their familiar buffalo roast, the trappers unanimously condemned the "tame beef" as being "too fat and downright sickening." In a desperate attempt to gain a compliment, Kipp gave a slice of the beef to one of the squaws, who according to her custom, ate separately from the men. After a few bites, even *she* declared the meat to be barely edible and returned to the lean buffalo.

The records of these early repasts usually show that rum and whiskey constituted more of a basis for celebration than did the banquets. Frequently, stores of liquor were held in reserve by fur company managers and dispensed only on special occasions—especially at Christmastime. On Christmas Day 1837, a group of slightly inebriated mountain men spending the holiday at Fort Laramie (known also in that year as Fort William) in present-day Wyoming decided to celebrate the season with a loud report from the private fort's brass cannon. In order to make the blast even louder, the trappers stuffed an old pair of buckskin pants and several worn-out moccasins into the muzzle of the big gun. When the cannon was finally touched off, the muzzle shattered into a hundred pieces as bits of britches and rawhide flew into the air and rained down on the astonished trappers. Several men were wounded, including the drunken gunner, whose leg was shattered by the backfire.

By the later years of the fur trade, in the 1840s, the practice of hunting wild game for huge Christmas meals had become well established among the mountain men. Long after the exodus of trappers from the Rocky Mountain West, the sport of hunting wild fowl and big game for the Christmas board remained popular among pioneers throughout the region.

As the mountain men made themselves familiar with the ranges and habits of game animals, the feasts became more elaborate. No thought was given to the possibility that certain species would be decimated in any given area, and game animals were hunted wantonly. Trappers who gained a reputation for hunting prowess were sought out as guides by wealthy sportsmen from the East or from abroad. One such individual was Sir St. George Gore, whose royal estate encompassed hundreds of acres in the Irish province of Connaught. He became enthralled with the romance of the American West, where he led extravagant hunting expeditions during the middle years of the nineteenth century. As a guide he employed the intrepid Jim Bridger, who became his close friend and drinking companion. On one hunting trip alone, Lord Gore loaded twenty-seven wagons of provisions for an extended expedition of one thousand miles through the Rockies. According to one account, Gore collected trophies consisting of more than two thousand buffalo, sixteen hundred deer and elk, and over one hundred bears—with no apparent concern for the environment. Jim Bridger was with him much of the time.

During one Christmas spent in the wilderness, Gore's party, including Bridger, feasted on huge quantities of wild game while dividing several kegs of prime Irish whiskey among the small party. While the liquor flowed freely, Bridger lifted his cup high and, in the tradition of the old mountain men, toasted the hunting exploits of his partner and himself. Meanwhile, fiddlers played and the party sang lusty songs of misdirected western chivalry.

Despite the lack of controlled hunting, not all of the old beaver men dined so luxuriously as Lord Gore and Jim Bridger during the holiday season. Often trappers would find themselves isolated in the Indian camps during the winter months, subsisting on what meager fare was available. Or they might find themselves alone, stranded in a blustery mountain pass or lost in some uncharted territory.

One such wanderer by the name of Bigelow found himself all alone in the Oto Indian country one Christmas. Hungry and hiding from roving war parties, Bigelow recalled years later his dissatisfaction with spending Christmas in such dangerous surroundings. Determined nevertheless to procure a Christmas dinner, he left his hiding place to go hunting.

> On Christmas morning, when I went out into the air, I beheld a flock of prairie fowls sitting among the trees on the bank of the river, and I am ashamed to say how my heart beat, and with what delight, after living so long upon tough wolf's flesh and scanty diet, I looked forward to the sensual joys of a roast worthy of Christmas.

> A grand looking cock was sitting just within reach of my bullet, but my irresistible, covetous desire to get two birds at once, induced me slightly to change my position. I trod on some dry twig that was hidden by the snow, it snapped under my foot, frightened the fowls, and the whole flock instantly flew off.

In regions of the Rocky Mountains frequented by scarlet-capped French-Canadian trappers, Christmas celebrations were even more colorful. As early as 1819, U.S. mountain men were cavorting with *les coureurs de bois* in winter quarters. On Christmas Eve of that year, several of these French *voyageurs* employed by the American Fur Company introduced their American counterparts to the traditional dance of *La Gineolet*. Adorned in paint and clothed in bison robes with bells on their arms and legs, the Frenchmen enticed the Yankee trappers into the merry frolic, which lasted well into the night. The dance caught on and eventually became a familiar scene on the fur frontier, not only during Christmas but at the famed spring rendezvous as well.

It was customary among the French-Canadian trappers to exchange rounds of kisses with their companions on midnight of Christmas Eve; both the Indians and the somewhat dumbfounded white trappers called Christmas "kissing day" in certain regions of the northern Rockies. The custom of exchanging gifts with their Indian allies was also widespread among the French-Canadians. In a ceremony known as the *feu de joie,* a large circle of bonfires was ignited in the center of an Indian village. The head chief of the village would be invited to sit in the center of the circle along with a representative from the trappers. Decorated skins would be placed in the circle. Indian families and individual mountain men would enter the circle, and in the frosty night air, they would place gifts of food and game or clothing on the skins. At the conclusion of the ceremony, the gifts would be distributed to their people by the headmen of both races.

If there was any semblance of organization to these early celebrations in the mountain camps, it came from the French Jesuit missionaries who frequented the Indian villages of the northern Rockies during the era of the fur trade. Many U.S. traders visiting the villages of the Nez Percé or the Flathead tribes were astonished to find residents speaking fluent French and sometimes celebrating Christmas in a near-Christian fashion. Although the liberalized bacchanalian lifestyles of the mountain men precluded most religious ritual, the Jesuits tramped the wilderness performing mass marriages for the trappers and their Indian women. One account tells of a zealous priest who married over fifty couples in a single camp on Christmas Day 1844. Recognizing only monogamous unions, the priest refused to perform marriages for trappers living with more than one squaw. Surely, if polygamy had been sanctioned, the number of ceremonies performed that day would have greatly increased!

By the waning years of the 1840s, the golden age of the Rocky Mountain fur trade was over. The mountain men had played their role. They had explored vast areas of untracked wilderness and brought back word of fertile valleys and rumors of gold that would entice a new wave of frontiersmen. They also introduced customs of Christmas to the young land. The practice of hunting wild game for holiday feasts, Christmas sporting contests, and affirmations of friendships with other cultures became familiar traditions to pioneers of later generations.

Taos, New Mexico, below the

Sangre de Cristo Mountains.

· Three ·

A Southwestern Navidad
1841

In a wide promontory below which the sparkling Rio Encebado empties into Rio Taos, a small shepherd boy wrapped in a sheepskin blanket lay on the ground gazing up at the heavens. The rarefied high-country air was crystal clear, and the brilliant Milky Way glittered like a chain of diamonds in an obsidian sky. The pungent scent of piñon logs burning in a small fire pit hung in the crisp winter air. The only sound was an occasional clanging of the bells lashed to the hemp collars around the necks of the few sheep in the boy's flock. Below, in the dark valley, candles burned on the deep-set window sills of time-weathered adobe dwellings. The boy could make out the huge bonfire blazing in the village plaza to honor the saints. Earlier in the day, a light dusting of snow had moved silently down from the sacred Sangre de Cristo Mountains and across the juniper- and sage-speckled desert. Amidst this tranquil beauty, the boy's heart beat faster in anticipation of the morrow. It was Christmas Eve—an enchanted night in an enchanted land.

It was 1841, and the carnelian hills, where small boys had tended their sheep for over two centuries, rose high above the earthen village of Taos. Situated in a country where the very hills and valleys spoke of antiquity, Taos was the pulse of the southern Rocky Mountains. Into this venerable country had come the intrepid Hernando de Alvarado in 1540, searching for gold. In 1598 the timeless land that would become New Mexico was subdued by the mighty conqueror of the Rio Grande, Juan de Oñate. The proud Pueblo Indian defenders all along the great valley had fallen easily to the guns and lances of the conquistadors. For two hundred years, the iron rule of the European overlords brought turmoil and suffering to the Indian people of the Rio Grande Valley. During this time, the Spanish and Pueblo cultures crossbred with each other, and elements of Christianity mixed with Native American customs and practices.

The little mud-hued villages in the north were visited by daring fair-skinned trappers. They came in search of beaver, penetrating the forbidden Spanish borderlands to trade their pelts at the Taos fairs. After 1821 the small trickle of American frontiersmen swelled to a flood tide as Mexico welcomed the Yankee trade caravans that plied the dusty Santa Fe Trail from Independence, Missouri to the strange land beyond the blue horizon. A few stayed, married Mexican women, and became respected citizens and leaders within the province.

By 1840, after a period of revolution and bloodshed, Taos lay on the far northern frontier of the politically distraught Republic of Mexico. The mingling of the Spanish, Indian, and Anglo civilizations had transformed the northern Mexican frontier into one of the most visibly cross-cultural regions in North America. And nowhere on the continent were the festivals and traditions of Christmas so rich and colorful as in New Mexico.

Undoubtedly, the shepherd boy who tended his sheep on that Christmas Eve in 1841 had witnessed the ancient festival of *Las Posadas* (The Inns) earlier in the evening. One of the oldest and most beautiful Christmas traditions in the Southwest, the symbolic pageantry of *Las Posadas* reenacts the journey of Mary and Joseph to Bethlehem and their search for shelter. The custom was introduced to Mexico in the sixteenth century by Father Diego de Soria and spread north with the Spanish frontier. The procession could easily have involved the entire community as the participants paraded quietly through the rutted streets of Taos, following the fortunate man and woman selected by lottery to portray Joseph and Mary. When the "room at the inn" was finally discovered, after knocking on the doors of many residents, the entire town would be treated to a gala fiesta. The church would be illuminated by burning crossed piñon logs carefully placed around the perimeter of the cathedral grounds in a tradition known as *Las Farolitas* (The Little Lights). Great platters of food—tamales, enchiladas, and wild game—would then be laid out on brightly colored blankets in the church square. Everyone feasted well into the night. After the fiesta, families would depart for their homes, where candles would be lit in the windows to burn throughout the night. The midnight mass and one on Christmas morning were the highlights of the Mexican Yuletide celebration.

Many of the Anglo transplants to New Mexico during this time adopted the Spanish-Mexican customs at Christmas. These people converted to Roman Catholicism, the dominant Christian sect in the region, and participated in the beautiful Christmas celebrations with enthusiasm. They also

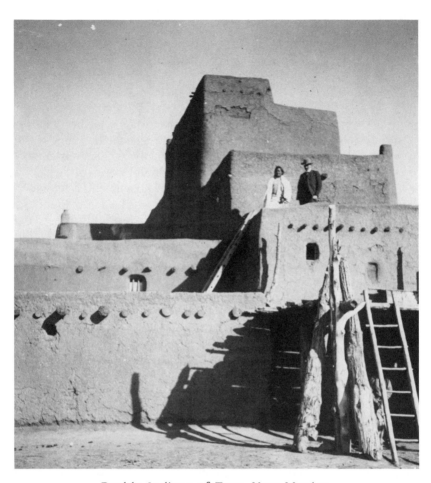

Pueblo Indians of Taos, New Mexico.
Denver Public Library, Western History Department.

introduced their own traditions to the Southwest, where those traditions blended with the earlier Spanish customs. Although the practice of decorating Christmas trees had not yet caught on in the United States in 1841, the craft of fashioning and adorning homes with boughs of evergreen was quite popular. During the middle years of the nineteenth century, pine garlands were to be found festively ornamenting doors and windows in the homes of U.S.-born frontiersmen living in Taos. The Mexican inhabitants of the Southwest borrowed the tradition, garnishing ancient Penitente crosses or beehive ovens in their modest adobe houses with fragrant spruce and pine from the nearby Sangre de Cristos.

The art of fashioning evergreens into wreaths was also catching on among families back in the "States" and was accepted into New Mexican culture, where local, homegrown materials were substituted when evergreens were not available. Red chilies in particular were shaped into circular wreaths to imitate the ones made of evergreen. More frequently, however, the festive dried peppers would simply be strung together in an elongated bundle known as a *ristra*. Placed beside doors outside houses, the colorful decoration festively complemented the weathered, red-shingled roofs that dotted the town. Sage, bear grass, and other desert plants were used to fashion small wreaths and other rustic decorations.

By far the highlight of the Anglo Yuletide throughout the States in 1841 was Christmas dinner. When imported to the Southwest, it quite naturally merged with the holiday fiestas and the cuisine of northern Mexico.

One of the most lavish Christmas feasts ever documented combined the best of northern Mexico's cultural platter. It was held at the ranch of a transplanted U.S. frontiersman. For several days before Christmas, young Mexican and Indian boys living in Taos were employed to hunt and trap wild game for the occasion. Other youths were sent into the mountains and adjacent communities to deliver invitations. These boys received an invitation to the great feast in return for their services. The anxious young shepherd who tended his sheep in the hills above Taos on that Christmas Eve was one of those lucky boys. To receive an invitation to the feast was considered a great honor. The host, after all, was one of the most respected citizens of Taos, a man of great deeds and almost a legend in his own time. His name was Christopher (Kit) Carson, and he was renowned among the old trappers and traders from the Missouri River all the way to the Rocky Mountains.

Kit Carson was born on December 24, 1809, in Madison County, Kentucky. He migrated with his parents to Boon's Lick, Missouri about 1818, where he enjoyed a frontier upbringing and became fascinated with the prospect of travel in the far West. At nearby Fort Osage in 1826, the seventeen-year-old Carson, nicknamed Kit by his teenage friends, joined up with a caravan on its way to northern Mexico. These were the very early years of the Santa Fe trade. Although he adventured throughout the Rocky Mountain West, Carson fell in love with Taos and eventually decided to make it his permanent home. He trapped for furs and scouted for the army throughout the vast country extending from the mighty Yellowstone River to northern Mexico, where he chose to stay. He befriended and cavorted with practically all of the famous mountain men during the heyday of the Rocky Mountain fur trade in the late 1820s and 1830s.

After the death of his Arapahoe wife, Waanibe, Carson was briefly married to a Cheyenne woman called Making-out-Road, who divorced him within a few months by tossing his belongings out of their tepee. By 1841 he was back in Taos courting the beautiful Josefa Jaramillo, the daughter of a powerful and politically influential Mexican family. Josefa was fourteen years old. Carson was thirty-two. Carson converted to Catholicism because of their impending marriage, a union that would elevate the scout to a position of political prominence in Mexico. Sometime before Christmas, Carson decided to throw the gala soiree on the frontiersman's ranch where he was spending the holiday season to celebrate his birthday, show off his future bride, and hold perhaps a last reunion of the old mountain men who symbolized the freedom of his youth.

The local runners employed by Carson to carry the word far and wide had done their job well. Carrying the invitation to nearby hamlets, other boys relayed the message north in a primitive, frontier "telegraph" line similar to the long-distance relay systems used by the Plains Indians, and early on Christmas morning the trappers started showing up at the ranch. Singly and in small groups they rode through light, powdery snow under a glaring cobalt sky. They had been on the trail for days, riding from their hidden camps on the Arkansas, the Platte—from as far away as the Big Horn and the Green. To the excited young boys who had spread the word, these fabled mountain men were every bit as valiant and noble as the medieval knights of old. Their names made the heart beat faster; Jim Beckwourth, Old Bill Williams, Bill Simpson, Jack McGaa, "Uncle" Dick Wootton, and others came in that day. They were outfitted in dun-colored buckskins with long fringes and brilliant beadwork—their *gage d'armour* and the pride of squaw workmanship—and it seemed they could be heard from far away as their fiery-eyed ponies cantered arrogantly in the bright Christmas sunshine. The obligatory heralding of great individual deeds, both real and exaggerated, sounded through the thin, high-country air as the mountain men appeared on the horizon. As their horses reared on their haunches and pawed the frosty air, they shouted their epithets rather like a Sioux or Cheyenne at a victory dance after counting many coup: "I'm the man that shot the Grizz[ly] that kilt the trader up at Fort Lisa" or "The Rocky Mountains is the mantle of the world and Chris'mus is today and Carson is the King."

The thunder of hoofbeats and the self-glorifying exclamations of these wolf-robed cavaliers of the backwoods surely filled the young boys and other passersby with awe. Great curiosity spread throughout the entire population of the Taos Valley, for here were assembled some of the most famous names on the frontier.

Jim Beckwourth, one of the few black trappers in the Rockies during this time, designated himself as official cook. Huge pits had been dug the day before, and a great variety of meats was prepared barbecue-style. Bear, venison, wild turkey, and buffalo cooked slowly in the coals or over a spit. The great favorite of the old trappers—the fatty tails of beaver, sliced and pickled—was prepared by Beckwourth as if he were an experienced French chef.

During the late morning, shooting contests were held among the trappers, to the delight of the local children. A fine shipment of Missouri whiskey brought to Taos during the summer furnished prizes for the winners, and small kegs of "Taos lightening," the locally made brew, served as awards to the runners-up. By 11:00 A.M. the guests from around Taos had begun arriving, bringing huge quantities of green chili, steaming corn tamales, and other Southwestern delicacies to add to the feast. The ranch house was elaborately decorated with red chili peppers and evergreens hung along the *vigas* — the rough-hewn log beams that formed the structural interior of the house. Amidst this ornamentation, huge tables had been set for the noon meal.

Kit Carson sat at the head table. On his right was his beloved Josefa, along with members of the Jaramillo family. Ceran St. Vrain sat to his left, as did Charles Bent, mastermind of the once successful trading partnership of Bent–St. Vrain and Company and husband of Josefa Jaramillo's older sister, the refined Maria Ignacia. Five southern Cheyenne chiefs "wearing their state uniform of headdress, paint and feathers," according to one eyewitness, were seated at a "second table" on the left, along with headmen of the Rio Grande Pueblo groups. The trappers were seated on the right and were considered equal to the Indian chiefs. There were many courses, mainly of lean meats. The delicate meat from the humps of buffalo was reserved for the head table. Cuts of lesser quality were distributed among the other tables, the least desirable cuts being relegated to servants, Indians under the status of chief, and the Mexican boys who had been invited. These individuals, considered to be of lower status, were seated outside on the ground in the fashion customary in the ancient caste system of Mexico — a system that was highly ironic in light of the strict code of frontier individualism embraced by the old trappers present at the dinner.

Over three hours were spent at the dinner tables. Many toasts were made. The quality of the wine and spirits was voted unusually fine. After the cook, Jim Beckwourth, became intoxicated, however, the "program was less formal." In fact, it became a raucous affair, with scant use of silverware on the part of the Indians and the free-roaming mountain men. By evening everyone present agreed that the Christmas festivities were "the greatest known to that date" in the entire Taos region and Kit Carson was "chief over it all." For the first time in recent memory, different races and Indian tribes had "ate, drank and smoked together." The last toast of the evening was one pledging "fraternal peace" among the races in the Taos Valley.

It would be idyllic and fitting to conclude that fraternal peace among the races endured after that Christmas Day 1841. Unfortunately, it did not. Within the next five years, Taos and all Mexico would be wracked with upheaval and war. With the victorious march of General Stephen Watts Kearney's Army of the West into Santa Fe on August 18, 1846, New Mexico passed into the hands of the United States as the Mexican War raged on fronts farther to the south. Kit Carson became a courier for the American cause, carrying military dispatches in this war that might result in the defeat of his wife's people. On January 19, 1847, a group of Mexican and Pueblo Indian patriots briefly revolted against the American conquerors in Taos, murdering military governor Charles Bent in the process.

Despite recurrent social and political strife, the rich cultures of the varied populations living in New Mexico continue to endure, distinct but yet harmonious. Perhaps in no other region of the United States do these cultures complement each other so well, especially at Christmastime, when the pageantry, the festivals, and perhaps even the ghosts of the old mountain men riding through the Christmas snow can still enchant the imaginations of small shepherd boys.

The Salt Lake Valley settlement

of Brigham Young and his

followers, circa 1870.

· Four ·

Christmas in Utah
1847–1858

Although the vast majority of pioneers immigrating to the Rocky Mountain frontier during the nineteenth century came as individuals or small family units lured by the hope of economic opportunity, one group of brave settlers came en masse for quite different reasons. The little band of pioneers who first beheld the valley of the great Salt Lake on July 24, 1847, had no vision of furs or gold but the dream to form lasting foundations that would be realized in one of the harshest environments to be found anywhere in the American West.

Persecuted by neighbors in the Midwest for their nonconforming religious beliefs, the group deserted first Nauvoo, Illinois, and then Independence, Missouri, for a new beginning in the barren wastelands west of the Rocky Mountains. Led by bold and resourceful men of insight, they platted one of the most beautiful communities in America. They were the Latter Day Saints—the Mormon faithful whose determination to build a new Zion in the sage-covered alkali deserts of the Great Basin was matched only by the hostility of the land they had to tame. Their success was made possible by the unusual organizational abilities of a man who was perhaps the West's greatest colonizer, Brigham Young. The lush green tree-lined avenues of Salt Lake City today stand as a monument to his ingenuity and perseverance.

The theocracy that emerged among these devout people represented the fortitude that enables man to conquer nature and institute lasting culture in the wilderness. The Mormons or "Saints," as they called themselves, were the first substantial group of Anglo-American pioneers to establish a permanent family-based population in the Rocky Mountain West. Consequently, they developed enduring customs of Christmas for the inland empire, and their colorful and sometimes elaborate celebrations would mix with traditions of other pioneers in the West and spread throughout the region.

Christmas was a popular holiday in the Salt Lake Valley, despite the physical and economic hardships experienced by the Saints. The early years, of course, were a time of trial. During the autumn months of 1847, the first harvest was so meager it was questionable whether or not the little party of brave pioneers would be able to survive the winter. Nevertheless, the faithful were determined to celebrate the Christmas holiday. Although stores of food were depleted and reasons for merriment limited, one Mormon pioneer in particular was determined to make the day one of thanksgiving. Lorenzo D. Young wrote of that first Yuletide in the Salt Lake Valley:

> I gave a Christmas dinner. Father John Smith, Brother John Young, Brother Pierce and their wives, and also Brother Jedediah M. Grant, Sister Snow and Harriet and Martha took dinner with us. After dinner Father Smith blessed our little Lorenzo. The occasion was a most pleasant one and the day was spent in social chat, singing, etc.

Most of the faithful spent that first Christmas working as usual. The earth had to be plowed and wood and sagebrush collected for fuel. On the day after Christmas, the pioneers collected at the flagpole of their crude little fort to sing praises to God and pray for sustenance in the uncertain times ahead.

Brigham Young spent Christmas 1847 back in winter quarters near present Council Bluffs, Iowa (intending to lead a second group of Saints across the plains with the greening of the prairies in early spring). By 1849 subsequent migrations had made the community relatively secure, and that year was considerably more enjoyable than the one two years before. The season's harvest had been substantial, and on Christmas Day a grand party was held at the home of Brigham Young. One hundred fifty of his followers were invited to the gala festival. "The tables were twice filled by the company," we read, "and all were feasted with the good things of the valley." "When the tables were removed, dancing commenced, which was continued with energy and without interruption, except for supper, till a late hour."

By 1851 the population of the new Zion had multiplied as a host of new converts crossed the plains, some walking the distance pushing hand carts loaded with their worldly possessions. Many of the newly arrived

Saints were from foreign nations. Naturally they brought with them rich traditions of Christmas from their faraway homelands, and their customs fused with the Mormon community celebrations. On Christmas Day 1851, a Teutonic brass band of twenty-six promenaded in the streets of Salt Lake City and played from horseback in front of the homes of prominent citizens. It is entirely possible that "Captain Pitt's Brass Band" conducted the first musical Christmas parade in the Rocky Mountain West. In future times the custom would take root in towns throughout the frontier and even find its way back to eastern communities during the early years of the twentieth century.

The celebration of 1851 was unusually elaborate because the community had prospered beyond the imaginations of its inhabitants. An early resident reported on the activities.

> Christmas Day. Fine weather prevailed in Great Salt Lake City. All the hands engaged on the public works attended a picnic party in the Carpenter's Shop on the Temple Block which was cleared and decorated elaborately for the occasion. Several hundred persons attended and enjoyed themselves in both dance and song. President Brigham Young was also present. The enjoyments were varied with songs and addresses. The brethren of the band serenaded the inhabitants of the city from midnight till daylight which was quite a treat.

In actuality, about one hundred forty-five people had gathered at Carpenter Hall, the largest community building in the frontier town. It was festively decorated with pine boughs from the nearby mountains. Another resident reported that "Merry workmen, with their happy wives, and smiling daughters clad in genteel apparel came pouring in [to Carpenter's Hall] from every quarter, loaded with an abundance of luxuries of every description." Brigham Young, now assuming the governorship of the territory the Mormons called the State of Deseret (honey bee state), rose and addressed the crowd. He congratulated the assembly on the current state of prosperity in the valley and gave his blessings to the people.

Throughout the nineteenth century, these festive Christmas parties became a tradition and were usually held at the Beehive House, the home of Brigham Young. After the guests left, it was customary for the Young children to hang their stockings on the ornate mantel above the huge fireplace. Gold and silver paper ornaments and strings of popcorn would grace the sitting room and, in later years, elaborately decorated Christmas trees. In the morning, Young's many wives and their children would find brightly wrapped parcels from John Halsam's pioneer department store under the tree and in their stockings. By this time the Youngs, and indeed most prominent Mormon families, celebrated Christmas much like any relatively affluent mid-Victorian-era American family.

By the 1850s, however, the ratio of non-Mormons to Mormons in the Salt Lake Valley was increasing. Congress formalized the territory and named it Utah (after the Ute Indians), despite the efforts of the Saints to have their home dubbed The State of Deseret. In 1857 Brigham Young was replaced as governor by the United States Congress, and twenty-five hundred federal troops under the command of Colonel Albert Sidney Johnston were needed to enforce the installation of a congressionally appointed non-Mormon governor.

Brigham Young ordered a number of his faithful followers to strike out to virgin lands in the West and establish new communities in order to assert the Mormons' political influence. The initial years of these new settlements, with the threat of starvation, were similar to those suffered by the faithful in the Salt Lake Valley during 1847 and 1848. Being essentially a communal society, however, produce was shared equally among the pioneers in times of hardship. During Christmas in the new communities and in Salt Lake City itself, extensive efforts were always made to care for the poor and indigent. Church groups were organized to make sure that all families had a good meal on the holiday. Very quickly in the history of the Great Basin, it became customary during Christmas week to provide both food and clothing to the Indians living near the Salt Lake Valley. In later years, this custom spread to new regions as the Mormons extended Christendom to the baked mud pueblos of the Hopi mesas and the lodges of tribes dwelling in the Idaho Basin. Indeed, it can be argued that the first instances of organized Christmas charity in the Rocky Mountain West began among the Mormon pioneers of Utah.

By the time of the great California gold rush and the rush of the fifty-niners to the Colorado gold fields across the Continental Divide, the Mormon faithful were well entrenched along the western slope of the central Rockies. As the little community at the base of the Wasatch Range grew and prospered, her people's rich and festive customs of Christmas would mix with practices brought to the mountains and valleys by gold miners hailing from both Europe and the East. By the decade of the 1860s, a host of culturally rich Yuletide celebrations had become well-established traditions throughout the Rocky Mountain West as the wilderness grudgingly retreated before the bold determination of newly arrived pioneers.

Part Two

IN THE
MINING CAMPS

DENVER'S FIRST CHRISTMAS CELEBRATION

Tapping the barrel and having a high old time.

· Five ·

The Queen City's
First Christmas
1858

Christmas day 1858 dawned bright and clear over the listless South Platte River, and the temperature began to climb above the freezing mark. As faint tendrils of white smoke began to ascend from the makeshift chimneys of several tents and cabins and to disperse into the thin, high-country air above dirty canvas roofs, a sleepy-eyed, bearded man began stirring a large pot of corn that was simmering on an iron stove in the corner of his simple log cabin. The dried corn, carefully rationed for the winter months, had been soaking since the previous day and was now being prepared as part of a great holiday feast.

Suddenly the man noticed something strange—a large dark object ascending rapidly to the top of the cast-iron kettle as the water began to bubble. It was a fat field mouse—thoroughly boiled. The man grabbed a handy spoon and carefully scooped out the unlucky intruder. There was only enough dried corn in storage to last the camp through the winter months. It could not be wasted, even because of a mouse in the Christmas stew. The man nodded in satisfaction after tasting the corn. His contribution to the Christmas banquet was ready.

The man's crude log cabin was located on a dusty, wagon-rutted strip of prairie that would eventually be named Fifteenth Street, and the unlikely chef was known in the dusty little mining camp as General William Larimer, founder of the ramshackle assemblage of hovels named Denver City.

Six months earlier, a party of Georgia prospectors led by William Greene Russell had washed a few hundred dollars' worth of gold dust from a small pocket west of the confluence of Cherry Creek and the South Platte River, at a spot called Dry Creek. As the news of gold in the Pike's Peak region of the Kansas Territory spread eastward to the Missouri River landings, a number of potential (if inexperienced) prospectors set out across the plains to what they thought would be the "New El Dorado." Soon adventurers from the East began arriving near the site of Russell's pocket and camped along the west bank of Cherry Creek. The unsightly collection of tents and log cabins that sprang up was soon organized as the town site of Auraria.

All through the summer of 1858, more and more prospectors filtered into the Pike's Peak "diggings." Among them was a party from Lawrence, Kansas Territory, which staked out the east side of the creek, naming it St. Charles. As members of the St. Charles Town Company rushed back to Topeka to gain a charter for their new community, another party from Leavenworth, Kansas Territory, arrived on the scene. Among them was William Larimer, a town builder of great ability, determined to bring needed leadership to the new settlements rather than to profit from gold. Larimer and his men decided to acquire the St. Charles town site on the theory that it had been abandoned. Later Larimer was accused of "claim-jumping," but because of his persuasive personality, he won his claim and became the recognized founder of Denver City, which was named for the ex-governor of Kansas Territory, James William Denver.

A few other camps sprang up in the immediate vicinity, including Arapahoe City, Plum Creek, Russellville, the short-lived Montana city, Curtis, and Spooner camps. In the minds of most of the inhabitants, all of these simple communities were merely winter quarters for the cosmopolitan collection of early migrants to the new gold bonanza. Most of the men had arrived late in the summer or fall, and there was not much time to look for gold before cold weather set in. Wood had to be cut along the river for shelter. Meat had to be acquired and dried. Buffalo, deer, and elk hunts were daily necessities. The shabby, scattered, rival camps along Cherry Creek and the South Platte were cut off, isolated for the winter. Their male inhabitants were in the middle of the wilderness, separated by hundreds of prairie miles from their families at Christmastime.

Christmas crept up very quickly that year. With preparations for the winter, the men on Cherry Creek had hardly noticed that "the season" was upon them. Many of the prospectors dreaded the very idea: "Christmas! What's Christmas to us? A million miles from home—from anywhere," was the general feeling in the camps.

Nevertheless, a few enterprising souls in the Spooner camp were determined to celebrate the holiday. Four days before Christmas, these enterprising men went through the camps organizing committees and planning a grand Christmas feast. Wild game in the region was plentiful and the proposed menu extensive. Fifty special guests from other camps were invited, including William Larimer, E. P. Stout, president of the Denver Town Company, and Samuel Curtis, the civil engineer who had platted out Denver City. The festival planners recognized the adept leadership that existed in the Denver camp and requested that speeches be given by some of its men. As a whole, the fifty-eighters were not a physically hearty lot, but were men of initiative and responsibility — it took initiative and sound planning to be among the vanguard on any new frontier of the West. The flotsam so characteristic of mining camp society was yet to migrate to the Pike's Peak gold fields.

When Christmas Day was upon them, the men drifted from cabin to cabin and throughout the several camps wishing each other "Season's Greetings" and inviting friends and strangers alike to the festival to be held that afternoon. Because the day was warm, many men lolled around discussing prospects for finding gold in the mountains next spring, telling jokes, and discreetly avoiding the bittersweet subject of loved ones "back in the States."

But the subject of family was very much on the minds of the isolated miners. According to an eyewitness account, one heartsick young man, when wished a Merry Christmas, broke down and vented his loneliness with the reply, "If I only knew how Annie and the baby are — to be separated on Christmas like this . . ." Another man replied, "I'd give my team [of oxen] for a letter."

The single men in the community, however, were determined to cheer up their comrades, and they engaged them in the preparation of Christmas dinner. The efforts were sometimes frantic as the inexperienced cooks feverishly attempted to coordinate their efforts in time for the afternoon feast. "More wine for the pudding sauce," shouted one man urgently as he popped his head out of a tent.

At last the time was at hand for the banquet. The menu rivaled those of New York's finest restaurants on that Christmas Day. There was buffalo, venison, elk, wild turkey, and prairie chicken. Vegetables included potatoes, beans, and of course General Larimer's slightly embellished corn. Desserts were plentiful, with dried fruits of all sorts, prickly pear preserves, and custard pie. There was whiskey and wine, lovingly brought across the plains for just such an occasion, and a local brew, delivered the previous evening by the ubiquitous New Mexican trader "Uncle" Dick Wootton and dubbed "Taos lightening." This had been spigoted into pans during the morning and set up on barrels where the men could easily fill their cups throughout the day.

After dinner a series of toasts was given to the new land, manifest destiny, and families and friends back home. Songs were sung, including one that was composed especially for the occasion:

Way out upon the Platte
Near Pike's Peak we were told,
There by a little digging
We could find a pile of gold.
So we bundled up our duds,
Resolved at last to try
And tempt old Madame Fortune,
But it's root, hog, or die.

The honored speaker for the day was William Larimer. As the waxing twilight extended its amber glow to the distant mountain peaks, the dignified leader of the Denver City camp rose from his seat behind a rough board table and began to speak. He told of rich strikes in the mountains and the potential for agriculture in the region. "There is wealth," Larimer boasted, "not only in the mines but in the soil. We have innumerable treasures, sufficient to justify immigration to the fullest extent." Predicting a glorious future for the new city, he proclaimed that "We have laid the foundation for a city, an outlet, for this gold bonanza and for the Rocky Mountain region."

The speech was prophetic. With the coming of spring, a swelling migration of adventurers crossed the plains to the Rocky Mountains. Rich ores were found in the canyons and mountains west of Cherry Creek, in Gregory Gulch and along the Blue River. New towns sprang up, and upstart Denver City grew to become the major service center for the new mining industry.

Although William Larimer, disillusioned by political misfortune, would leave Denver in 1864, the process he envisioned on that Christmas day in 1858 endured beyond his wildest dreams. Denver was blessed in its early years with leadership of unusual ability. Men like S. S. Curtis, William Byers, David Moffat, Jr., Jerome Chaffee, Bela Hughes, Luther Kountze, Amos Steck, and others together insured the success of the new city in the far land. By June 1870 a spur line of the Union Pacific Railroad arrived from Cheyenne, followed two months later by the first locomotive of the Kansas Pacific. Denver became the hub of the Rocky Mountain region, supplying the mining camps to the west and developing a viable agricultural hinterland to the east. Within two decades, it was transformed from the crude "turnstile town" known to those participants of its first Christmas celebration into one of the most important metropolises of the West. Although more than 125 Christmases have gone by in the Queen City since that one in 1858, to many later inhabitants of Denver, as well as to those of 1858, the real meaning of that Christmas, or for that matter any Christmas, was hope for a successful future.

Colonel Samuel Curtis believed in that vision. Perhaps remembering another promise for the future made centuries before and symbolized by a bright star shining over a humble stable in the ancient Judean hills, Curtis proposed a Christmas toast: turning his head toward the heavens, he lifted his metal cup on high and said, "Westward the Star of Empire takes its way and now hangs bright over the Rocky Mountains."

Cabin near Vasquez Creek.

Colorado Historical Society

· Six ·

A Rocky Mountain
Turkey Shoot
1860

As the Pike's Peak gold rush spread to the nearby foothills from its humble beginnings along the banks of Cherry Creek, many Christmas customs made their way into the Rocky Mountain empire along with the cosmopolitan population. The mining camps attracted adventurers from all geographical regions of the growing nation, as well as immigrants from many foreign lands. Although the isolation of the frontier brought few creature comforts during the Yuletide season, old practices were fondly remembered in the days preceding the joyous holiday. Traditions were modified, using existing resources to the extent possible, and introduced to the new western mining camps. As the irregular mining frontier spread north from the central Rockies of Colorado into the regions of Montana, Idaho, and Utah during the 1860s and 1870s, so did Christmas customs.

One of the most widespread customs to emerge from the forests of the early colonies and find its way to the Rockies during the later nineteenth century was the institution of the "Christmas Turkey Shoot." From the Tidewater and Piedmont regions of the continent, American frontiersmen brought the tradition across the Appalachians during the eighteenth and early nineteenth centuries and had extended its practice to the Rocky Mountains by the eve of the Civil War. The initial survival of pioneers in this vast wilderness of varied topography depended heavily upon the hunting of wild game. Skills in marksmanship were a necessity but became a source of pride and esteem as well. Naturally, the frontiersman took advantage of community get-togethers to test his prowess with a gun.

Christmas became the most popular time of year to test one's shooting skills, and a holiday meal was offered concurrently at the local Christmas turkey shoot. (The custom has survived to the twentieth century. American Legion posts and other civic organizations sponsor the holiday contests in the form of trapshoots, with the prize being—of course—a fully dressed holiday bird.) During frontier times, however, the tradition took the form of either hunting live birds in the wild or shooting at birds tethered to a tree or a stake.

The first recorded Yuletide turkey shoot in the Rockies took place in the isolated mountain park of California Gulch near modern Leadville, Colorado, in 1860, and it was one of the most bizarre events of its kind to ever take place on the western frontier.

Following closely on the heels of the first gold strikes, a host of expectant and hearty men migrated to the new bonanza of the Colorado gold fields during 1859 and 1860. They quickly flooded the region with dingy, isolated camps dotted throughout the vast mountain strongholds on both sides of the Continental Divide. After stocking up on provisions in Denver City, the miners filtered up the canyons to the west, exploring rich placers in Gregory and Russell gulches. The crude, rough-hewn towns of Central City, Black Hawk, Nevadaville, and others soon speckled the landscape adjacent to Clear Creek, creating hideous scars in the pristine mountain canyons of the Front Range. Soon the prospectors emerged into South Park, panning for surface gold and creating unsightly pick-and-shovel towns like Tarryall, Fairplay, Hamilton, and Buckskin Joe. Across the Continental Divide, gold was soon being extracted by homemade rockers along the banks of the Blue River where Breckenridge eventually sprang from the gravelly soil.

One of the most ignominious collections of shanties and canvas tents among these early gold camps was Oro City, situated in the shadow of Mount Elbert in California Gulch, near the spot where boisterous Leadville would soon be built. During the spring of 1860, hundreds of prospectors were in the gulch panning a rich placer that briefly stimulated one of the largest intraterritorial mining rushes during Colorado's early years. Among the first arrivals to California Gulch was an energetic young storekeeper by the name of Horace Tabor, a man destined to become a United States senator and one of the dynamos of the Rocky Mountain mining industry during the nineteenth century.

After a long summer of arduous work, the snows came early to Oro City. By late October, the drifts piled up several feet against the log and board shanties, and gold panning came to a virtual standstill. By the middle of December, many of the men in the camp had begun thinking about Christmas and what, if any, celebration could take place in their isolated community. Anything elaborate was out of the question. Supplies like flour had to be hauled over Mosquito Pass, and even beans and bacon had to be brought in from Denver City. The weather was miserable, and it was doubtful that any supplies could make it through before December 25. It was agreed that any celebration would have to take place in the combination boardinghouse and saloon, a crude log structure in the middle of town. The ramshackle establishment was operated by an eccentric, bearded ex-trapper known only to the miners as "Old Newt." Would Newt even be concerned about recognizing the holiday?

After conferring with the unkempt saloonkeeper, the men in the camp awoke one frosty morning to find several handpainted placards posted around the town proclaiming:

**SHUTIN FOR TURKEYS
NEWT'S SALOON CHRISMUS EVE**

According to Horace Tabor, "Excitement mildly expressed the state of feeling." Many of the miners in Oro City were experienced frontiersmen, and the anticipation of participating in one of their favorite Christmas sporting events was well received.

Old Newt, however, was made the butt of numerous jokes by many of the more knowledgeable citizens of the crude mining camp. According to Tabor, "No one in the know believed for an instant that he had any turkeys or could get such a fowl nearer than Denver and that was certainly out of the question," and "the wild turkey was not to be found so far north."

Nevertheless, a sense of excitement spread throughout California Gulch in anticipation of impending holiday dinners. Newt had posted his signs in nearby camps as well, and a few days before Christmas a delegation from the Tarryall camp visited the saloonkeeper, proposing to find out once and for all if Old Newt had actually procured a bevy of the delectable birds for the advertised event. Confidently, Newt invited the men into his back storeroom. Accompanied by half the population of the diggings, the saloonkeeper opened the wooden door of the wobbling shed. The Tarryall committee stooped and quietly walked through the low entrance. There, along the back wall of the musty, smelly room, protruding through the slats of some homemade wooden crates, were the featherless red heads of at least a dozen wild-eyed gobblers. Satisfied, the delegation went away to spread the news far and wide.

As the pink alpenglow on Christmas Eve began to descend over the mountain peaks flanking California Gulch, men began to gather from all directions at Newt's Saloon. The miners were instructed to line up outside the dining room door, which was freshly decorated with evergreens. They were to be admitted one at a time, after payment of five dollars for three shots at the turkeys. Usually, the whole bird was tethered in the open, and rifles were used at considerable distance in the event. Newt's rules of the game were somewhat different. The turkeys were placed in a thick, bulletproof wooden box, with only the head protruding through a small slot in the barricade. Each man was to use his own revolver at a distance of twenty feet, shooting at the small head.

Newt, along with two of his assistants, had considerable trouble keeping the anxious miners lined up outside the dining hall. Everyone tried to crowd the door for a peek inside. The contestants were to remain outdoors, being admitted to the room one at a time to take their turns. One impatient young man at the front of the line boastfully stated that "he could already smell his Christmas dinner roasting." Horace Tabor was in line for his chance at a Christmas turkey. Many years later, he related what happened next. The following account is in Tabor's own words.

At last they got in line and the first man was admitted. "Bang!" There was a cheer as the shot resounded through the hall. Evidently, however, he had missed, for the waiting throng heard a muttered curse. Bang! The listeners heard a triumphant shout and then loud curses, mingled with Newt's voice, evidently in expostulation. He had gone around and come in the back way. Next the second man was admitted and the first did not reappear. This time the shot evidently took effect, for we heard a triumphant cry, followed by the same curses and subdued laughter. The third was admitted with the same result. Then the fourth and the fifth, and so on until ten of the solid miners had been admitted. But, strange to relate, none of them reappeared with their turkeys to tantalize the less fortunate ones. The crowd began to grow suspicious. They pressed forward more and more eagerly until when the door was opened to admit No. 11 all made a rush and surged through and into the dining-room. They rushed forward to where the box was, and there, with its deceitful head was [the carcass of] a miserable turkey-buzzard. You know that the head of this horrible vulture is so formed and colored that any good old Christmas gobbler would take it for his own.

When this discovery was made, the back door was thrown open to all. There in the kitchen, the crowd met up with the first ten contestants, along with Old Newt. The proprietor's withered and toothless face was red as a tomato as he slapped his knee and literally made himself dizzy with mad laughter. The first ten contestants were, likewise, laughing uncontrollably as they witnessed the expressions on the faces of their comrades in the room. Just outside the back door were seven more carcasses of the odious scavengers that had been hit by the "lucky" shooters. Eventually, all of the men in the crowd began to laugh out loud.

When the chaos finally subsided, Newt related the source of his innovation. He told the dumbfounded miners how he trapped the vultures in

Middle Park a few days before Christmas, with the help of some small Ute Indian boys. Each of the successful contestants had, of course, been angry when he found out the true identity of his intended holiday feast, but each had agreed, in the spirit of the season, not to spoil the fun.

Although many "legitimate" turkey shoots would be held at Christmastime throughout the West in future years, the resourcefulness of the one held in Oro City in 1860 was long remembered by the camp's pioneers as making Christmas memorable for the lonely inhabitants. The first round of drinks was on the house, and the revelry lasted until the early hours of Christmas morning. Everyone left the saloon in high spirits, including Old Newt, whose good fortune, both convivial and financial, increased considerably on that long-ago Christmas Eve in California Gulch.

A western family of the Victorian
era with their Christmas tree,
a source of obvious pride

Buckwalter Collection,

Colorado Historical Society

· Seven ·

Gingerbread and Chintz
1870–1893

T he nostalgic vision of Christmas past is nowhere more stylized than in the image of sparkling snow on the evergreens of quaint Victorian villages of the Rocky Mountain mining frontier. A glowing, candle-lit Christmas tree casting its warmth through thickly paned windows and chintz curtains in a colorfully adorned gothic house in the mountains is as representative of our western Christmas as Charles Dickens's London is of the English Christmas. Inside the home, a roaring fire illuminates the plush velvet furniture and rich, burnished woodwork, with yards of fresh pine garlands and red satin ribbons. A beguiling little girl with long, flaxen curls might sit in her lace dress, lost on a posh fainting couch, watching the snow outside and eagerly contemplating the arrival of St. Nicholas. In the parlor richly hung with flocked wallpaper, the fragrance of burning pine and aspen logs subtly stimulates the senses of those within. The spirit of the Yuletide is almost electric — excited but unspoken and reverent. This was the Victorian Christmas — the stuff that dreams are made of.

By the decade of the 1870s, the gold mining industry in Colorado was firmly established and moving north into the virgin territories of Idaho and Montana. Soon silver would replace gold as the principal mineral extracted from the Colorado mountains. During the very early years of any new strike, individual prospectors could make a modest living washing gold dust from the banks of mountain streams with pan or rocker. After the surface placers played out (typically within a few months), the rich veins of ore that brought millions in revenue were tapped through the use of scientific mining processes. These veins were usually situated deep within the hillsides. The discovery of surface gold usually did not bring quick wealth to the ordinary prospector. Indeed, the extraction of ore required a heavily capitalized enterprise and expensive machinery to obtain, crush, and process the precious metal. These requirements were compounded when silver became the goal of the enterprise. Only those individuals who had the business sense to incorporate and purchase the necessary equipment could afford to speculate in the giant subterranean mines. The independent prospector bent on quick fortune was forced out of the system, having to either move on to a newly reported strike or work for poverty wages in the employ of the exploiting mining companies.

When corporate mining took over in the mountains, the rough-and-tumble shanty camps took on an air of semipermanence as new gold or silver kings established year-round homes on the sites of their newly found fortunes. There they built the ornate Victorian houses with elaborate cupolas and mansard roofs so familiar in the Rocky Mountain mining frontier. Designed from plans published by eastern architects in popular magazines, the homes could be as simple or as elaborate as the tastes and financial resources of the homeowner dictated. With lumber from the mountains plentiful, local sawmills processed trees by the thousands into lengthy clapboards characteristic of the architectural style known today as carpenter gothic. Elaborate gingerbread latticework was fashioned by careful hands to complement the exteriors of the flashy houses. This ornamentation came to symbolize the newfound wealth.

As the established mining towns grew and prospered, they attracted a host of "urban pioneers"—bankers, storekeepers, and professional people who came west to profit from miners rather than from mining. These nouveaux riches of the mining West brought their wives and children to their gaudy new homes in the hills, and it was the women of the mining frontier who eventually tamed the raw state of existence found in the early camps. They instituted social service agencies, art, and culture in the prospering communities. They also showcased the trappings of Christmas on a scale unparalleled outside the large cities of America.

Considered today to be one of the best-preserved mining towns in the Rockies, the venerable village of Georgetown witnessed all the wistful opulence commonly associated with the luxurious celebration of nineteenth-century Christmas. Founded as a gold camp during the initial years of the Colorado gold rush by the brothers George and David Griffith, Georgetown settled into the steady production of silver after R. W. Steele first discovered rich ore in 1864. By the 1870s, the community was appropriately dubbed the "Silver Queen" for the numerous rich mines in the

vicinity. Very soon the town became dotted with brick business establishments and baroque Victorian cottages trimmed in whimsical gingerbread.

Typical of Georgetown's self-made millionaires was grocer Virgil B.
Potter. Striking it rich after investing in the productive Colorado Central
mine, Potter added a thirty-five-thousand-dollar addition to his modest
hillside cottage in 1889. Sold to Frank A. Maxwell in 1893, the Maxwell
House is today recognized as one of the ten outstanding examples of
Victorian architecture in the United States. Complete with cupola, distinct
mansard roof, and dormer windows, the house stands as a testament to
the combined ethics of ostentation and utilitarianism exemplified during
the late nineteenth century.

The Potter residence, and indeed all similar homes in Georgetown,
would likely be trimmed at Christmastime with pounds of fresh evergreen
and ivy, carefully attached to thin wire and hung around entranceways,
picture frames, mirrors, and fireplace mantels. Of course, a huge Christmas
tree would adorn the parlor where family and friends would surely congregate around a crystal wassail bowl placed on an expensive grand piano
to sing traditional English carols on Christmas Eve. Stockings would be hung
over the fireplace before retiring in anticipation of the arrival of Santa Claus.

By the early 1870s, family gatherings with morning church services
and elaborate Christmas dinners were already replacing the community
festivals and sporting contests common in the early years of the mining
camps. To be sure, a turkey shoot would be held on the day before
Christmas, and the northern European custom of tramping the hillsides
for a Yule log large enough to burn through Christmas Eve and Christmas
Day might still form the foundation of community activity, but the par-
ticipation in such events became drastically reduced in the later years of
the mining industry. As the mining towns took on trappings of stability,

the local merchants came to play a central role in the increasing trend toward commercializing Christmas. As early as 1872, Georgetown's local newspaper, the *Miner,* reported:

> Monti & Guanella, agents of Santa Claus in Georgetown, are preparing to fill all orders for Christmas goods promptly, and to the entire satisfaction of their customers. The innery old gentleman flashing over the country with his capacious freight teams, has cramed [sic] the large store of his favorite agents with turkies [sic] and chickens, gobbling and cackling, to grace Christmas feasts. And then such quantities of vegetables, fruit confectionary, cake and toys for little girls, blushing maidens, stately dames, little boys and old boys, as the jolly old elf has on exhibition at his headquarters at Monti & Guanella's is a sight entertaining and highly satisfactory to the inhabitants of the "Silver Queen."

On Christmas morning, it was customary for wealthy mining town residents and their families to attend church services. Although saloons continued to outnumber churches in most mining communities (including Georgetown), where families were present, the women insisted on establishing places of worship in addition to their other cultural activities. With the help of itinerant clergymen, such as Father Joseph Machebeuf and John Dyer in Colorado, as well as others throughout the Rocky Mountain West, these enterprising women helped to make the church a familiar fixture in stable mining towns.

One of the oldest churches standing today in the Rocky Mountains is a direct effort of Methodist Clara Brown. An ex-slave, "Aunt Clara"

"Aunt Clara" Brown
Colorado Historical Society

worked as a washerwoman in the sinful days of Central City, Colorado, to save enough money to bring other blacks to the West. Christmas services were frequently held in her ramshackle house, until she persuaded other parishioners to pledge funds for the construction of a stone church. Central City's Saint James Methodist Church was well attended at Christmastime and frequently became the scene of community festivity. In 1885 the *Rocky Mountain News* reported that the Methodists held a Twelfth Night celebration and dance, which featured as its guest of honor and representative of the Grand Army of the Republic the former Methodist preacher Colonel John M. Chivington, perpetrator of the infamous Sand Creek Massacre in 1864.

After the Christmas church service, residents of Central City, Georgetown, Leadville, Virginia City, and scores of other mining towns throughout the Rockies would adjourn to their homes to partake of elaborate Christmas dinners, featuring roast goose or turkey and fine wines and liqueurs. Imported oysters were one of the most popular and sought-after delicacies in the mining towns at Christmas (and during the year). In fact, several newspapers of the 1870s described Christmas trees in local saloons and dance halls decorated entirely with fried oysters. After dinner, weather permitting, it was customary to go ice-skating. On Christmas Day in 1885, the *Rocky Mountain News* announced that in Black Hawk, Colorado, "several hundred lovers of skating enjoyed ice skating at the rink Christmas nite for the first time this winter." Also in 1885 in Leadville, "Mr. C. C. Hopkins gave a fancy exhibition of riding on a bicycle" at the ice rink in front of hundreds of holiday skaters on Christmas Day. After the exhibition, women in long, black dresses and fur muffs sallied forth upon the ice arm in arm with mustachioed men elegantly dressed in wool coats and fur "Cossack hats."

Parties and community cultural events were more common during the week after Christmas than on the holiday itself. Operas or plays were quite frequent, in addition to community dances. Newspapers reported in 1886 that the Christmas Ball (held on December 26) sponsored by the Patriotic Order Sons [of the] America in Black Hawk was attended by over 165 couples. During Christmas Week 1885, the Broad Opera Company of Denver presented "*The Mikado*" at the [Central City] opera house where the populace [had] the opportunity to witness Gilbert & Sullivan's latest popular opera presented in a first class manner."

These scenes of idyllic opulence that have come to characterize the Victorian celebration of Christmas in the picturesque mining towns of the West were not shared by all. For every mining magnate, there were hundreds of others who did not share the bounty. Some women who came west during the mining rushes were without the support of wealthy husbands to subsidize their efforts to bring culture to the frontier. Losing their men on the road west or in mining accidents, many women found themselves alone, earning a living as best they could in the bustling mining communities.

Mrs. Nathan Collins was one such woman. Arriving in Virginia City, Montana, during its early years, Mrs. Collins found herself caring for her chronically ill brother, while supporting herself where food and supplies had to be freighted in from San Francisco. Flour sold for "$110 per sack of one hundred pounds, Potatoes, $36 pr. bushel and eggs, $2 dozen." Taking in sewing and laundry for pennies, the determined young woman barely made ends meet. One Christmas morning, Mrs. Collins opened the creaky door of the little cabin she had built herself and found lying in the snow against the side of the door a sack of flour with a small card attached. On the card were the words, "Merry Christmas from the miners, in rememberance [sic] of your kind acts and cheerful words." Mrs. Collins later recalled that "this proved to be but an initial kindness shown me by these men, and during the remainder of that long, severe season our home was made quite comfortable and our stock of provisions kept fully adequate to our needs by means of the money I was able to earn with my [sewing] machine and their occasional gifts."

By the late 1880s, the corporate mining structure that had evolved needlessly exploited the mine workers in their employ. The "company town," in which the hard rock miner worked long hours for low wages in unhealthy conditions, literally indentured many souls to the corporation management in an unregulated labor market. Many of those unfortunate individuals were recent immigrants to the United States, eager to share in the reputed opportunities of the "land of the free." Christmas offered little for them save the chance to drown their sorrows at the numerous saloons that were open on Christmas Day. In 1885 the *Rocky Mountain News* naively reported on the activities of Cornish miners during the time that their employers were merrily ice-skating with their families at the Black Hawk rink.

> The Central City brewer says that more beer was sold in Central City Friday than on any previous Christmas since beer was manufactured here.
>
> The Cornishmen, or a good many of them, are still celebrating. They are having Christmas long drawn out. All day yesterday and last evening the principle [sic] beer halls were filled with Cornish miners who were treating themselves generously with beer, and made the large halls resound with Cornish songs which could be heard all over town. The Cornishman takes more than a week to celebrate Christmas. He begins with Christmas Eve and keeps it up till New Year's Night.

Although the pioneers were quick to adopt the rich Christmas traditions of foreign immigrants to the Rocky Mountains, it would take years before they fully understood the basic needs and concerns of the foreign expatriates.

With the great silver crash and the financial panic of 1893, the golden days of the Rocky Mountain mining empire came to an end. Fortunes were lost almost overnight. Many individuals never recovered. Quaint Victorian mining towns rich with traditions of Christmas slid into a long period of decay and abandonment. Few relics of their opulent past remain, and today they are remembered at Christmas as vestiges of an idyllic age glowing with romantic images that inspire old-fashioned Christmas cards. An idyllic society? Perhaps in our nostalgic reminiscences, but it was in fact rooted in arrogance and ostentation.

Part Three

ON THE PLAINS AND MESAS

· Eight ·

Snowbound
1855

For many of the earliest settlers on the Great Plains, the advent of a prairie blizzard could be life-threatening. When such a storm came blowing in on Christmas, the holiday was no time for repast and thanksgiving. Frequently a pioneer family's most vivid Christmas memories brought to mind no images of tranquility and festive celebration. Indeed, the greatest gifts at these times were often far more basic. Despite the mythical image of individualism attributed by later generations to the pioneer, it was more often cooperation among neighbors and even strangers of different persuasions that could mean the difference between life and death on the frontier.

In the years immediately preceding the Civil War, the newly formed Kansas Territory (1854), which extended to the Continental Divide of the central Rocky Mountains in what is now Colorado, became the laboratory for "popular sovereignty," the perceived right of white settlers democratically to decide for themselves whether or not they would permit the insidious institution of slavery within their borders. This great dichotomy of those for and against slavery touched off ill feeling and bloodshed in Kansas even before the giant volunteer armies of the Union and Confederacy were conceived.

During the 1850s, before the Homestead Act, most "squatters," as they were known in Kansas, preempted land in the unsettled, fertile, and timbered river bottoms, believing no one could survive out on the open prairies. Near the frontier settlement of Osawatomie, in Miami County, where squatters of antislavery, or "free-soil," persuasion were migrating, the Thomas family took up a claim and built a crude, unchinked log cabin from the oaks and cottonwoods along the creek they would call home in the new land.

In the late autumn of 1855, Reverend C. Robert Rice from Tennessee came to Miami County. The son of a southern "aristocrat," Rice had recently been ordained into the southern wing of the Methodist church. Reverend Rice had come to the frontier to organize missions among the Indians and to secure a preaching circuit among the new settlers then filtering up the river and stream valleys. In the memoirs he wrote years later for the Kansas State Historical Society, the clergyman noted that riding west from the site of the great Shawnee Mission, the grandest of the Methodist Indian missions, he was "in a strange land, surrounded by . . . very strange people. I had never seen an Indian before," Rice remembered. "My feelings were indescribable as the naked-shouldered redskins gathered about me extending their hands."

That night Chief Baptiste of the Peoria tribe extended his hospitality to Rice, making him a bed of "buffalo robes and woolen blankets before an open door" of a lodge. After some initial evangelical work among the Peorias, the clergyman spent Christmas week of 1855 in the white settlements. On the old military road, near Chouteau's Trading Post, Rice married his first couple. But most of the free-soil settlers nearer his destination of Osawatomie were not so quick to request the services of this southern preacher. In Osawatomie Rice made his way to the cabin of another Methodist man of the cloth, Reverend Samuel L. Adair. An ardent antislavery man, Adair told Rice bluntly, "We don't want you here; you have been sent by the southern church to help the Missourians make Kansas a slave state." Rice later discovered that Adair was married to the half sister of Osawatomie's most radical abolitionist, the fiery John Brown.

Assuring Adair that he was "no politician" but was in Kansas only to preach the gospel, Rice rode on to the nearby homesteads searching for a congregation to listen to his Christmas sermon. On December 22 he came upon the Thomas homestead. Although Thomas was a free-soiler, he welcomed Rice into his home. "I asked the man [Thomas] if I could spend the night . . . with him," Rice remembered. "He looked at me for some time, and then asked, 'Are you a preacher?' I said, 'I have preached some, and expect to preach occasionally if the people will hear me.'" Thomas asked the clergyman if he would preach a Christmas Sunday service, and Rice heartily agreed.

Rice stored his saddlebags and overcoat in the cabin. In the afternoon he was sitting by the open door studying his notes for his Christmas sermon, while his host cut firewood and his host's son rode out to notify other settlers of the impending Yuletide service. But "just before the sun went down," Rice recalled, "a sudden gust of wind came from the north and made the cabin shake. In a few minutes Mr. Thomas . . . came in with a 'back log' for the fire and with a shiver said, 'I never saw it turn so cold so fast in my life.'" Rice dropped his books and went to help his host carry in more firewood.

The wind and cold increased every minute. "Some of the upper crevices between the logs of the cabin had been filled with twisted hay," Rice remembered, "and in a little while they began to fall out and the north wind came in with a rush and roar. Soon the snow was coming in too, covering beds and everything else in the cabin." Thomas suggested the warmest place to weather the storm would be in bed, and by morning the snow was three inches deep on the beds and floor. It had to be swept into piles in the corners of the cabin. The snow had piled up outside to the eaves of the cabin. "The whole heavens were literally full of snow," Rice wrote.

Suddenly the men remembered their horses and Thomas's livestock outside near the haystacks, in the teeth of the storm. It took most of the morning to dig tunnels out from the door of the cabin, which had been drifted shut, to the endangered animals. "Our horses would have been covered with [snow]," Rice claimed, "if they had not trampled it under their feet. We had a job getting the packed snow from under them and piling it up around to protect them as much as possible from the cold wind." Several times during the day, the men had to leave the cabin and clear away snow and ice from the faces of the livestock so the animals would not smother. That night Rice remembered pulling himself into a small knot and wishing he had never heard of the Kansas Territory.

The next morning it was still snowing, and there was more than a foot of new snow. Again the men had to tunnel through the drifts to save the animals. Soon it was apparent there would be no Christmas service because other settlers were also snowbound. "It was Christmas eve," Rice noted, "but we had no merry gathering, no Christmas tree, no plum pudding! We made no effort to have a Merry Christmas . . . I did not try to preach a Christmas sermon . . . for I could not feel any Christmas or New Year's spirit in the cold air. I never heard 'Merry Christmas' or 'Happy New Year' once. The people I met, as well as myself, were not in a merry mood. We were enduring a bitter cold winter."

Christmas Day dawned with "blue sky and bright sunshine, but a very cold wind from the north." After a good breakfast, Reverend Rice saddled his horse and made a start back to Osawatomie, convinced the Kansas Territory was not habitable.

The memory of that terrible holiday season of 1855 remained in the mind of Reverend C. Robert Rice all his life. On that long-ago Christmas in territorial Kansas, Rice learned, although years later, that sometimes the greatest gifts of all on the frontier were gifts of survival. After the storm, settlers across Miami County counted heavy losses among their livestock. Thomas's livestock could easily have perished if it were not for the extra help given him by the visiting circuit rider.

At such times, it was not uncommon on the frontier for political differences, and even spiritual concerns, to be put aside in favor of more urgent mutual needs. Within a short time, politics would tear "bleeding Kansas" asunder. In 1861 Kansas would enter the Union as a free state. Some of its western lands would be severed to help form the Colorado Territory in the same year. Settled principally by Kansas free-soilers, Colorado, too, would remain loyal to the Union during the Civil War. Reverend C. Robert Rice's experiences in frontier Kansas, including the lessons of Christmas 1855, must have made an impression on him. The southern gentleman remained in Kansas and lived to see it enter the age of the automobile and the electric light. As late as 1906, he was living in Hartford, where on March 9 of that year, he and his wife, Lucy, celebrated their golden wedding anniversary.

Life in the saddle could be very lonely.

Christmas celebrations brought a welcome change.

From a drawing by Frederic Remington, Denver Public Library, Western History Department

· Nine ·

Ranch Festivities
1878–1893

Although a wide array of Christmas customs came west with the mining frontiers of the Rocky Mountain empire and became refined in the gothic mansions of that industry's self-made millionaires, nowhere was the celebration of the holiday more spirited than on the huge ranches of the feudal cattle barons. Both great and small ranchers from all economic levels knew how to celebrate the Yuletide in style. Because they were so isolated on the rangelands, Christmas was a time for reunion and fraternity with neighbors and family, as well as an excuse to dine extravagantly. From the legendary Matador Ranch in Texas to the frozen ranges of the Bosler spread in the Rocky Mountains, the open-range cattle industry of the post–Civil War years created new millionaires who rivaled the lords of the mining empire in their displays of extravagance—especially at Christmastime.

Beginning with the first herds of longhorns that made the long drive up the dusty Chisholm Trail to Abilene during the late 1860s, money was to be made in the open-range cattle business. On the open range during the early years, several thousand animals would keep as well as one. Feed and water were essentially free, and if a rancher could walk his beef to the railheads, he could sometimes realize huge profits. By 1881 booster literature like James Brisbin's *The Beef Bonanza: Or How to Get Rich on the Plains* helped attract both Eastern and British capital into the business.

Farmers moving westward imposed quarantine laws on the importation of Texas longhorns during the tick season, and the center of the industry shifted from Texas and the raw Kansas cow towns to the northern ranges of Colorado, Wyoming, and Montana, beyond the head of the Goodnight-Loving Trail. By requiring their cowboys to preempt free government land and turn it over to the ranch owner (or risk being blacklisted), the cattle kings of the Rocky Mountain West were successful in building huge land empires. By the mid-1880s, these nineteenth-century "barons" ruled their feudal estates by the law of the six-gun and the ruthlessness of the medieval aristocracy. To protect their interests and insure that the ranges remained open, they frequently organized huge syndicates. One of the most powerful of these "rangeland mafias" on the northern plains was the Wyoming Stock Grower's Association. By the 1880s, the organization had gained control of all livestock affairs in Wyoming Territory. Using their power and authority to harass potential competitors among small ranchers and homesteaders, whom they categorically labeled as "rustlers," the association employed merciless stock detectives to drive "undesirables" from the ranges at gunpoint.

Despite their hardfisted image, the cattle kings of the Rockies knew how to display their material wealth. At Christmastime the huge celebrations staged on their ranches rivaled any in the West. Christmas Day might start with a traditional turkey shoot near the massive stone ranch house. If the weather was warm, the Yuletide feast might be held out in the open; if not, the large dining room would accommodate the numerous guests, who would sit on oak benches scattered around massive stone fireplaces. Beef, turkey, and wild game might make up the fare, in addition to fine wines and such sumptuous delicacies as oysters and lobster imported on the railroads—at considerable expense—to keep the seafood fresh. Wranglers and other employees would be welcome at the house for the occasion.

A huge evergreen, freshly cut in the mountains, might be decorated on Christmas Eve by family and ranch hands. Standing in the stately living room, the tree would be decked with strings of popcorn and cranberries, crepe paper balls, and candles in small brass-clip holders, counterbalanced with small lead balls. Christmas presents would be mail-ordered months in advance, which meant a mandatory trip to Cheyenne or Billings prior to Christmas to retrieve the gifts. During their trip to town, ranchers would also stock up on candy and baking supplies for the holidays.

The chief activity of the ranchers' Christmas was an elaborate dance on Christmas night. For many of the ranch hands, the gala party was anticipated throughout the year. Mrs. J. C. Underwood of Cheyenne recalled a Christmas dance at the ranch home of her father Donald Clark, a pioneer stock raiser in Wyoming's Horsecreek Valley.

Old and young, even little children and babies, came from Horsecreek, Chugwater, Pole Creek and Iron Mountain, and the festivities lasted all night. The small fry were put to bed in a huge bedroom while their elders danced and visited sometimes till well past dawn.

Fiddlers provided the music, and many contemporary square dance steps, as well as the time-honored Virginia reel, were enjoyed at these dances. In isolated areas, where the ratio of women to men was small, many wranglers improvised. Though it was not unusual for a cowboy to travel hundreds of miles to fetch a lady for the Christmas dance, more often the drovers would "draw straws," and the loser would tie a scarlet bandanna around his right arm and assume the part of the female in the dance. The practice was widely accepted, and no one thought less of any cowboy who "danced the dame's movements."

In ranching areas where a nearby town made community get-togethers easier, local cattlemen would congregate at a schoolhouse, hotel, or saloon for their massive private parties. In 1878 a Christmas dance was held at a local schoolhouse in frontier Rock Springs, Wyoming. D. G. Thomas, an old buffalo hunter for the Union Pacific Railroad, was present and recalled how local ranchers and miners enjoyed the festivities. On the day before Christmas, a delegation of men drove a buckboard into the hills and retrieved a twelve-foot pine tree. The evergreen was decorated by the entire community on Christmas Eve so that it would be ready for the dance. By early evening on Christmas Day, people started arriving at the schoolhouse. The men had kept the big iron stove burning throughout the day. The children of the community provided literary and musical entertainment for the grownups. Thomas remembered over a half-century later the children's eyes

sparkling with merriment and anticipation, and their voices ringing like silver bells as they sang the anthems and choruses. When Santa Claus came down the chimney their happiness was complete; the little candles were lighted on the tree, and the gorgeousness and the splendor of the ornaments and the wonderful presents on display were simply dazzling and wonderful. . . . After the Christmas tree and the entertainment came the dance. John Ludvigsen, with his music box, furnished the music on the accordion which he purchased in Norway, and it was truly a wonderful instrument. The quadrille was the principal dance, and the way the dancers whirled through the seemingly intricate figures was wonderful. I still believe that for sheer fun and enjoyment, the old-fashioned quadrille is far ahead of modern dances.

That Christmas dance in old Rock Springs lasted well into the night. It seems that the American cowboy of the nineteenth century was as much concerned about his music as is the modern westerner, who should take note that the early ranch land Christmas dances served as prototypes for modern country-western shuffles.

Of course, the weather on the northern plains was unpredictable and could spoil the Yuletide celebration during any given year. Mrs. J. C. Underwood told of one such catastrophe. A sudden blizzard stalled the train to Cheyenne, and guests did not arrive at the ranch in time for Christmas. The large family spent the day snowed-in and alone. Undaunted nevertheless and determined to keep the "Christmas Dance alive," after dinner they "rolled up the rug in the living room and danced with one another, Mr. Underwood playing the violin and the current resident schoolteacher the piano."

Despite their institutionalized intolerance of farmers and the homestead principle, there were occasional ranchers who felt sympathy for the bold determination of the "squatter" to carve a home from the rangelands of the Rocky Mountain West. Many small stock raisers allied themselves with the homesteaders in their fight against the corporation cattlemen. By the late 1880s, the cattle kings could perceive that their days were numbered. Unusual blizzards and cold temperatures, beginning in 1886, all but ruined the heavily capitalized ranches. But more important, by that decade a virtual army of hopeful pioneer farmers was sweeping across the western prairies. It would be the grim determination of the "sodbuster," driven by the promise of free land and new opportunities, that eventually would overcome nature's obstacles and conquer the great West.

A beautiful example of friendship between homesteader and small cattleman involved a young son of a modest rancher in the upper Pecos River country of New Mexico. Years later the unnamed lad recalled how an unexpected Christmas Eve blizzard swept their ranch.

As the little boy jumped into his upstairs bed and pulled a giant wolf skin over his blankets to await the arrival of Santa Claus, he heard a knock at the front door of the house. Peeking over the rough board loft to the downstairs parlor, the sleepy boy glimpsed his mother opening the stubborn door against the wind. A shivering young man stumbled inside. With tears in his eyes, he looked at the concerned woman and said, "One of our children is very sick, and if you will, I'd like for you to take it in out of the cold and do what you can for it." "Sure," the kindly woman answered. "Bring the child and its mother in."

This small family, fresh from the East, was homesteading and seeking their claim. They had become disoriented and lost in the storm.

When Christmas Day dawned and the ranch youngster ran downstairs to get his stocking from in front of the fireplace, he heard a woman crying in the spare bedroom. He went to the kitchen, where his mother was working. She told him that the baby had died during the night and that its mother was crying in the bedroom. The family dressed the baby and prepared it for burial. Some of the cowboys on the ranch made a tiny coffin from the rough pine boards of "a box Arbuckle coffee came in." Funeral services were held in the living room, and the ranch hands carried the little coffin through the snow to a grave they had dug on a knoll in the horse pasture. There they lowered the coffin into the grave with two ropes. Years later the unnamed little lad who awoke on that bygone Christmas Day to the harsh realities of the western frontier remembered:

> It was a sorrowful sight to see that father and mother when the time came for them to continue their journey to their new home, leaving their little one behind, buried there on the lone prairie. And ever after, when I hear that old cowboy song, "'Neath the Western Skies," I can see that father sitting on the spring seat of their wagon as they drove away, looking back at that little grave.

Herding cows could be cold work.

From a drawing by Frederic Remington, Colorado Historical Society

· Ten ·

The Cow Camp
1878

I f the powerful cattle barons of the Rocky Mountain West were the
feudal aristocracy of the open range, the solitary cowboys whom they
employed were undoubtedly the serfs. Hired by the big cattle companies, these hearty young men were paid low wages for the dubious
privilege of mending fences or riding drag at the dusty end of the trail
drive. Life always held potential danger. The possibility of sudden stam-
pedes or rustlers running off cattle was ever present. Black and Mexican
drovers were usually paid a few dollars a month less than Anglos for the
most dangerous jobs. There was nothing inherently romantic about being
a herder of cows. And the cowboy ranked low on the social scale of the
nineteenth-century West. Nevertheless, his daily needs were provided for
by his employer. Fed and sheltered by the cattle outfits, the drover had
time to establish a personal relationship with his environment, and a love
of nature was one of his most enduring pleasures.

The winter months might find him alone or with only a few companions in a desolate line camp at the far reaches of his employer's land.
With little to do but turn back the neighbor's animals and track down
strays, the cowboy only broke the monotony by drinking, playing cards
with his comrades, or simply thinking. No wonder most of these stoic
men were quiet and shy when they suddenly found themselves thrust
into civilization's complex web. Harsh winters could find them stranded
in their shacks on the windblown ranges for weeks on end, perhaps at

Christmas. A favorite subject of the cowboy artist C. M. Russell was the loneliness of the isolated drover at Yuletide. With whiskey bottle held on high amidst the endless panorama of starlit sky, sagebrush, and snow, there was little the solitary cowboy could do to celebrate the holidays.

Yet this isolation to some degree tempered the desires and needs of many a cowboy to include the more meaningful things in life. The animals with which he worked became dear to him. The beauty of the land, the spring rains that gave the sage-covered range its fresh aroma, the smell of black coffee and saddle leather all took on special meaning—and so did the message of Christmastide. Although modern literature has mythicized him, the one emotion that accurately characterizes the American cowboy is sentimentality. That wonderful Victorian mood idyllically associated with small children was very much a part of the lonely cow camp of the West. Despite the hazards of the trade, the sentimental cowboy might risk his life to capture the spirit of Christmas on the open range.

During one harsh winter on the northern plains in the late seventies (probably 1878), three resolute cowboys did just that. Their parallel stories of privation and determination at Christmastime illustrate the extremes to which the "knight of the plains" might go to honor the Yuletide, however simple the celebration might be.

In the far reaches of the open rangeland of southeastern Wyoming Territory, William Francis Hooker and his older partner, Nick Huber, were assigned to "line" duties in a small dugout "with gunny sack doors," along La Bonte Creek in what is today Converse County. There the two men settled in to face King Winter, undoubtedly charged with the dull task of patrolling the far boundary of some enormous spread to turn back strays. Nick, a Bavarian immigrant, would celebrate his sixty-fifth birthday on December 25.

The only visible landmark that broke the untamed landscape was solitary Laramie Peak, sixty miles in the distance. The nearest site of civilization was Fort Fetterman, forty miles from the cow camp. Having no calendar to mark the days, the two drovers kept track of time as well as they could by scratching lines on the sod walls of their rough dugout.

As the relentless winds of December began blowing the dry snow into dirty, billowing drifts along the rises of the broken terrain, the two cowboys began to reflect upon the approaching Yuletide. They agreed it would be great sport to ride over to Laramie Peak and cut a Christmas tree. After careful consideration of the potential hazards Mother Nature could offer at that season of the year, the partners decided to throw caution to the wind in an attempt to keep Christmas. Nick would start the long ride to Laramie Peak with first light in search of an evergreen. Meanwhile Bill Hooker would journey to Fort Fetterman to purchase needed supplies and perhaps a few bottles of "Christmas cheer" to make the lonely holiday a bit more tolerable. The two wranglers set out in freezing temperatures toward their destinations. By late afternoon an ominous bank of pewter clouds obscured the western horizon and extremely harsh winds began to sweep across the barren rangeland. The two humans were reduced to insignificant specks of faint movement amidst blowing yellow sand and tumbleweeds.

At about the same time that Bill Hooker and Nick Huber set out on the blustery plains for their Christmas pilgrimage, another cowboy who was over one hundred miles to the southeast, near the pine-bluffs country of extreme western Nebraska, kissed his young wife and three little ones good-bye. Wrapping a long woolen muffler around his face and tucking its long trailers into his heavy canvas duster-coat, the hopeful wrangler mounted his four-year-old Appaloosa and galloped off into the impending storm, along the trail to Cheyenne. As his wife waved her handkerchief from the door of their log cabin, she noticed that her husband's sun- and wind-weathered face, hardened and wrinkled from spending rugged years in the out-of-doors, made him seem far older than he was. This particular winter, to stave off his loneliness, the man had brought his wife and children to the modest cabin that was used as a remote line camp during the bleak months for pioneer ranching activities in the vicinity. Despite their isolation, the cowboy was determined to give his family a proper Christmas.

By eight o'clock that evening, Bill Hooker had reached Fort Fetterman. After stocking up on needed provisions, including "coffee, salt, needles and thread," he purchased three bottles of good rye whiskey from the military post's sutler. Just as he was ready to leave, however, something else caught his eye. On a sudden impulse, the sentimental drover purchased a shiny new skinning knife from the merchant's glass and oak display case as a Christmas present for his partner, Nick Huber. Bill left Fort Fetterman that evening. He traveled a few miles and then spent the remainder of the night shivering under his saddle blankets along a dry creek bed. The only shelter he found was under some leafless box elder trees that lined the stream bank. The Stygian, dark night was bitter cold.

A few hours before Bill Hooker left Fort Fetterman, the young wrangler from the pine bluffs sighted the brightly painted wood-frame buildings along the Union Pacific sidings in Cheyenne.

The storm front moved in during the night with full fury, and by morning four inches of new snow had fallen across the southern Wyoming rangelands. There was no sign that the storm would let up. Bill Hooker knew he had to keep moving to keep from perishing. He was an expert tracker and knew he could find his way home, unless the winds stirred up ground blizzards. Even without the storm, the trip back to the line camp would have been slow because Hooker was packing over sixty extra pounds of supplies. But the cowboy made fairly good time with the wind at his back. Finally, about midnight, he spotted the crude dugout shored up with old wood crates and cowhides around the front door. The snow had stopped on the return trip. But in its place was the relentless wind accompanied by dangerously cold temperatures. The moon traced a gossamer filigree of hoarfrost on the sooty window of the dugout as Bill Hooker removed the crates in front of the door and entered the relative warmth of the earthen shelter.

To Bill's complete surprise, his partner, Nick, was already back at the dugout. He was fumbling around in the darkness trying to light an oil lantern as Bill entered the dwelling. In the corner of the tiny room was a small but fine-looking pine tree that Nick had obtained on the slopes of Laramie Peak. Aware of the impending blizzard, Huber had cut the tree and ridden straight for home the previous night. The tree was already decorated with paper flowers made from red, white, and brown soap wrappers.

While Bill Hooker was traveling home through the snow, Nick whittled a small whistle and a "jumping-jack" from wood scraps with his jackknife as presents for his partner. An apprentice toy maker in his native Germany, Nick Huber had not forgotten his trade. Bill presented the new skinning knife. The rye whiskey was broken out, and both men celebrated Christmas amidst the great empty void of Wyoming's winter landscape, safe, at least this time, from the elements on the other side of their makeshift door. Outside the dugout, the unforgiving wind howled around the shelter.

Death was always a close companion during the nineteenth century. The winter months in the Rocky Mountain West could be cruel and unforgiving, testing the fortitude of the strongest frontiersman. Those individuals living close to the land had to organize long in advance, arduously preparing for months of hardship, sickness, and isolation. An impromptu journey on horseback could prove deadly. To make such a journey, one had to be highly motivated.

As the cold orange globe of the winter sun ascended over the rolling plains, revealing puffs of blowing snow spiraling off miniature cornices at the tops of huge drifts, a two-horse sleigh silently moved through the still Christmas landscape. A small family had left Cheyenne to visit some ranching friends east of town. Sighting an incongruous speck of color in the stark white landscape, the driver halted the sleigh. He stepped down and trudged the forty yards or so to a small gully, where he found the frozen corpses of the young Nebraska cowboy and his Appaloosa. Apparently, the man had been heading east toward the pine bluffs country. Tightly clasped in his frozen arms was a torn burlap bag filled with a few pitiful Christmas packages, their bright tissue paper wrappings ripped by the victorious wind. And lashed across the saddle horn on the frozen horse was a miserable branch of a scrub pine tree.

The spirit of Christmas? Certainly it existed on the rolling plains of the West. Despite the boredom and isolation, the never-ending, backbreaking work, the pioneer would find some way to celebrate the Yuletide —

even if at risk. Innovation was frequently required, and determination was a necessity. But the determination to capture the spirit of Christmas was nevertheless epitomized in the monotonous confines of forsaken line camps inhabited by sentimental cowboys.

· Eleven ·

Good Neighbors
1880

Christmas on the sod-house frontier was often a bittersweet time. It was the point in the grinding year when both farmer and rancher took stock of the past season. Often the reckoning was not good. Drought, crop failure, prairie fires, a deflated market for beef, even grasshopper plagues, could mean there was little cause to celebrate during the holidays. When subzero winter temperatures and prospects of a life-threatening prairie blizzard loomed on the unbroken horizon like a murky specter, problems intensified and became more immediate.

Contrary to the usual impression, at these times of extreme need, farmers and ranchers often set aside their differences to lend each other a hand. This sharing was especially visible at Christmastime during the lean years of the 1880s. From Dakota to New Mexico and eastward across the rolling mid-grass prairies of Kansas and Nebraska, the spirit of Christmas was displayed repeatedly on the lonely plains of the American West.

At the beginning of the decade, the year 1880 was especially severe, a dark harbinger of worse things to come. A cycle of drought gripped the high plains that summer, causing crop failure from Texas all the way to the Canadian border. The scarcity of grass on the open ranges worried the cattlemen as their animals approached the winter in less-than-good shape. For many people, as well as livestock, there was not enough food. When a string of unusually severe blizzards struck the plains in early

December and settlers were cut off, kitchen pantries and storage cellars became bare alarmingly fast.

Throughout the plains, local communities organized relief committees through which ranchers and homesteaders who had food to spare put aside their differences and contributed what they could to the greater need. From miles around, settlers congregated on the ranches and in the little towns where relief services were likely to be provided. One story tells of a young eastern Colorado farmer who was homesteading with his brother and his wife, who was suffering from tuberculosis. Too proud to ask his immediate neighbors for help, the determined young homesteader traveled eight miles on foot through the deep snow to a ranch where it was rumored a relief committee had been formed.

Obtaining what food he could carry, the man immediately began the long journey home. It was the day before Christmas. Within a mile of his soddy, however, the man fell in the snow from exhaustion. He rested only a few minutes because the wind had begun to blow fiercely from the north, whipping up a near-blinding ground blizzard. When he started on the last leg of his journey, the proud farmer was too exhausted to carry the bag of food any farther. Reluctantly, and not without a brief fit of rage, he dropped the bag in the snow and proceeded toward his sod house. After another half mile, the man fell again in the snow but this time was spotted by a neighbor, who put the man on his finest bay horse, escorted him home, and provided enough food for the family to last out the blizzard.

The local newspapers for December 1880 also told of a young wife who started out through the snow toward Denver on the family's aging sorrel mare to obtain food and medicine for her husband, who was stricken with pneumonia. Caught in a blinding snowstorm, the woman surely would have perished had it not been for a group of cowboys who were headed for Denver to obtain relief. They discovered the woman lost on the prairie and escorted her into town. Much to the relief of her ailing husband, she returned home in time for Christmas, escorted part of the way back by the same cowboys.

One Nebraska squatter appeared at the door of Mark Coad's American Ranch on the South Platte during the same storm. Coad later reported the ensuing conversation to a reporter from *Field and Farm.* "I have a family of ten persons," the homesteader told him. "We have eaten the last mouthful of meal and breadstuff. We have no potatoes or meat, and have had nothing to drink for two weeks except sassafras tea without sugar. Will you let me have a little [food] until I can get some from the relief committee." This young farmer had over one hundred acres under culti-vation the previous summer, but his entire crop had failed, and his family was near starvation. While the farmer was talking with Coad, some of the boys at the ranch brought in a freshly killed antelope; the squatter took home a hind quarter to his hungry wife and children.

Not all were as lucky as these. The newspapers also told the story of a man homesteading on the south fork of the Republican in Kansas who traveled eight miles to obtain sustenance from a neighbor. When he arrived at the neighbor's dugout, he found the man, his wife, and several small children all dead, their bodies frozen in their beds. Not a morsel of anything to eat was found in the house.

Indeed, throughout the plains the grim stories were the same. Wranglers were found frozen to their saddles after the blizzard, and whole families who had gone to bed to escape the cold were found frozen. For those who survived, livestock, including horses, pigs, and calves, for days shared quarters with humans inside the confines of musty sod houses. When the thaw finally came, the continuous dripping of mud and melting snow through the straw roofs of the soddies combined with a biting animal stench to make the dwellings uninhabitable for weeks. In many instances, cowboys persistently had to chip ice from the heads of horses and cattle so the animals would not suffocate.

For many ranchers, the worst was yet to come. The more publicized winter of 1886–1887 was especially hard on the big outfits, as cattle by the thousands froze to death on the open range. Yet for many of the old-timers, the December storm of 1880 was the one they most vividly remembered all their lives because it hit during the Yuletide. Christmas on the frontier had always been a time for reflection and planning. In times of hardship, the settlers of the plains did what they had to do to survive. To that end, Christmas became a time for standing fast and formulating new resolve.

The waving fields of western grain seen today extending from horizon to horizon like a sea of gold and the ranches, both large and modest, endure as a testament to the settlers' perseverance and success. Those who stuck it out were responsible for no less than taming the frontier and building a great nation in the process. But for many who lived on the frontier through the winter of 1880, the most cherished Christmas memories were of those simple acts of charity and goodwill that occurred when rancher and sodbuster buried their differences and gave each other a hand on that long-ago Christmas Eve on the Great Plains.

Snowbound travelers, circa 1906.

Colorado Historical Society

· Twelve ·

Christmas Travelers
1878

T hroughout the last half of the nineteenth century, the day before Christmas was a time for travel in many parts of the growing nation. During the golden age of steam, mighty express trains would speed excited passengers along iron rails to reunions with loved ones in front of the Christmas hearth. To be sure, rail travel at Christmastime was crowded and boisterous in the more populated regions of the country. It seemed that everyone aboard brought baskets of food, sugar confections, and an unusual number of packages tied with bright ribbons. Each gift would be "appropriately" decorated with paper cutouts of ice skaters, beautiful young maidens outfitted in white furs, or perhaps Old Saint Nick himself, laboring under a huge bag bulging with toy drums, horns, and china dolls. The chorus of "God Rest Ye Merry, Gentlemen" would be caroled by inspired children at every rail station along the Atlantic seaboard or in the heartland of the Ohio Valley. The crowds reveled in merriment and excitement as they sighted their loved ones stepping down from elegant palace cars. Reunited, families were quickly whisked away by omnibus or open sleigh through the frosty countryside, along frozen ponds and secluded woodlots. Later, nestled in the bosom of a favorite uncle's festively decorated parlor or anteroom, they would celebrate the jubilant Christmastide in lavish comfort under mistletoe hung from crystal chandeliers.

In the West, however, these familiar sights of joy and anticipation were not so common. Although some attempted long journeys, great distances often restricted family reunions on the frontier. In addition, weather and other natural hazards could abruptly spoil the holidays, despite the best laid plans of the Christmas traveler.

Conditions were especially risky along the high plains corridor that lies within three hundred miles of the Rocky Mountains. In that vast expanse, distance combined with the ever-present wind to wreak havoc with Christmas travel for many unfortunate pioneers. Even today, unpredictable and relentless prairie storms, accompanied by gale-force winds and blinding ground blizzards, can soar out of the Rockies or sweep down from Canada to strand travelers during the very height of the holiday season. Time stands still. The modern traveler, like his pioneer ancestor, must take heart, make do, and view the predicament as an overland adventure. The spirit of Christmas is not unknown on the windswept prairies. In fact, one of the most touching tales of Christmas involved six wayfarers, attempting a holiday journey on the high plains of eastern Colorado in 1878, stranded on a Kansas Pacific train.

The snow had already begun to swirl around the yards and the car-barns in Russell, Kansas, on the early morning of December 24, 1878, when the conductor shouted "All aboard." A small woman wearing old clothing stepped up to the passenger car. With her were two small children, tightly bundled and mittened and still shivering from their long wait on the plank-board platform.

They entered and took places on an oak seat in the rear of the coach. The woman barely noticed the three men already on board the train. Across the aisle was a "drummer," a traveling salesman on his way home to Denver after resupplying his stock of notions in Kansas City. In front sat a sad-looking cowboy, his face weathered and his hands scarred from years on the open range. Next to the cowboy was a conspicuously wealthy ranch owner. He was clad in an expensive sheepskin coat and high-peaked Stetson hat. His flowing moustache and high cheekbones gave him an air of elegance and strong character. There were no other passengers on board the train—the Denver Express, pride and joy of the Kansas Pacific line, had pulled through Russell the day before. Adorned with lavish Pullman sleeping cars, the express had been full of holiday travelers on their way to Colorado. This modest train carrying six passengers was a small "plug." Accommodations consisted only of a baggage car, a smoker, and one coach. It was the last train to Denver before Christmas and was scheduled to arrive late on the night of December 24.

As the small train pulled out from the station, the passengers introduced themselves. Their names have since been lost to history—they are not important. The woman, it was learned, was a poor widow who had taken up homesteading somewhere on the Kansas prairie. After the untimely death of her husband, she had attempted to keep the little farm going. She struggled through the drought and grasshopper plagues on the plains during the mid-1870s. Finally, giving up on the farm, the widow tried to make ends meet by moving first to Hays City and then to Russell. She took in sewing and labored at other odd jobs. At last, she gave up the unequal struggle altogether and was returning to Denver to live with her mother, also a widow. She told her male companions that she planned to start a small business. She hoped to borrow one hundred dollars in the city to use for rent on a storefront. She hoped the loan would be repaid within a reasonable amount of time.

When the train crossed into Colorado, the snowstorm intensified. Soon it became obvious that the passengers would not arrive in Denver in time for Christmas Eve. In fact, it was likely they would not make it at all. By afternoon the storm had worsened to a wind-driven blizzard. Finally, at a deep cut in the road, the locomotive plowed into an enormous drift created by blowing snow. The engine belched a last puff of white smoke into the frosty air and came to a complete stop.

The passengers were told they would have to spend the night on the train because the engine could not move. Immediately, one of the crew started on a dangerous journey of several miles up the road. His destination was a telegraph relay station, where he could call the snowplow from the Denver branch of the line. Resigned to their unfortunate situation, the passengers moved to the front of the car, where they sat around the wood-burning stove to keep warm. Outside, the snowstorm showed no sign of abating. The wind blew at gale force, driving the snow in sheets and filling the cuts with high drifts.

As the pale yellow, foreboding disk of the winter sun began to descend below the treeless, unbroken horizon, the threadbare little children began to cry despairingly. They could not be comforted—they had anticipated a joyous Christmas with their grandmother in Denver. A Christmas tree had been promised, as well as a few presents from Santa Claus. It was to be their first "real" Christmas. They were devastated by the blockade. Fortunately, their mother had brought along a basket of fruit. At least her children, and the men as well, did not want for lack of food.

After darkness fell, the men "tipped up two of the seats, placed the bottoms sideways," and with their overcoats "made two good beds for the little folks." Just before the small urchins were about to fall asleep, the drummer looked sadly at the others and said, "We've got to give those children some Christmas!"

"That's what," stated the cowboy.

"I'm agreed," added the rancher.

"Madam," said the drummer, "we are going to give your kids some Christmas."

"Yes, children," the rancher exclaimed, "Santa Claus is coming round tonight, sure. We want you to hang up your stockings."

"We ain't got none," quivered the small girl, " 'ceptin' those we've got on, and Ma says it's too cold to take 'em off."

"I've got two new pair of woolen socks," stated the rancher enthusiastically, "which I ain't never wore, and you are welcome to 'em."

"But Santa Claus will know they are not our stockings, and he will fill them with things for you instead," the little girl cried.

"Lord love you," retorted the burly rancher, "he won't bring me nothin'. One of us will sit up, anyway, and tell him it's for you."

The excited children then knelt down on the rough floorboards of the passenger car beside their bench beds, and with the first words of "Now I lay me down to sleep," three hats instinctively came off. The men's eyes welled up with tears. After the children were asleep, the men renewed their conversation. "What should we give 'em?" was the major question.

"It don't seem to me that I've got anything to give 'em," stated the cowboy regretfully, "unless the little kids might like my spurs . . ."

"I'm in much the same fix," said the rancher. "I've got a flask of prime old whiskey here, but it don't seem like it's very appropriate for the occasion, though it's at the service of any of you gents."

"Never seen no occasion in which whiskey wasn't appropriate," said the cowboy.

"I mean't ain't fit for kids," the rancher barked, handing over the flask to his companions.

"I begun on't rather early," remarked the cowboy while taking a long snort, "an' I always use it when my feelin's is onsettled, like now."

"Never mind," the drummer said. "You all come along with me to the baggage car."

Off the men trooped to the back of the train. The salesman opened his trunks and laid out before them a vast array of "glittering trinkets." The drummer looked at the others. He was wearing a broad smile. "We'll just pick out the best things from the lot," he said, "and I'll donate them all."

"No you don't," said the cowboy. "My ante's on this game, an' I'm goin' to buy what chips I want, an' pay fer 'em, too, else there ain't goin' to be no Christmas around here!"

"That's my judgment, too," said the rancher.

The men spent what seemed like hours picking over the merchandise, choosing the little presents they wished to purchase. The train crew caught the spirit of the season also, so that all hands went back to the coach with a load of delights to put in the children's stockings. They filled both socks until they bulged. And then they filled up two of the coach seats with even more gifts. The mother was crying.

When the men were finished arranging the presents, the train engineer surveyed their handiwork, scratched his head, and remarked, "We've got to get some kind of a Christmas tree."

Two volunteers immediately donned scarves and heavy coats and set out in the zero-degree temperature, through blowing drifts. It had stopped snowing. A bright moon shone on a blanket of white, snow-covered ground. It seemed to the men that they could see for miles across the moonlit terrain. No evergreen was to be found on the lonely prairie. Eventually, however, the two men returned to the train with a "good-sized piece of sage-brush," which they solemnly installed at the front of the car. The mother decorated it with pieces of colored tissue and assorted baubles from the drummer's depleted stock of notions. Finally, the crewmen placed brass train lanterns around the base of the improvised "tree."

By that time, the men were far too excited to sleep. Thoroughly captivated by the spirit of the season, they stayed awake all night. Each man secretly wished to be the first to witness the expressions on the children's faces when they awoke to find what the cowboy called the "layout."

Later on Christmas morning, the youngsters told the men it was the best Christmas they ever had. An impromptu service was held in which the woman sang "Jesus, Lover of My Soul" from memory. Everyone chimed in. After the hymn was finished, the cowboy twirled his hat in his leathery hand and stated with a shaky voice, "It feels just like church. Say, I'm all broke up; let's go in the other car and try the flask again."

By early afternoon, the train hand who had gone for help returned to the stranded locomotive. With him was the snow brigade from Denver. But even more important was the whole cooked turkey he had brought with him from the telegraph station. The stranded passengers and crewmen sat down and enjoyed a fine Christmas dinner in the coach.

By late afternoon, the snowplow had completed its job, and the train pushed on into Denver under clear skies. By the time the plug arrived at the depot, the mother had become "flushed with unusual color." The gratitude she felt for the kindness of her generous traveling companions was overwhelming, though her thoughts turned to her mother waiting for them at the depot, and she dreamed of the little business that, with some luck, she would be able to start in the city.

Before leaving the train, however, one more gift was presented. During the night, the men had assembled a "monsterous [sic] red plush [photo] album," purchased jointly by them from the drummer. In grand Victorian style, they had all autographed the ornate volume. Each man had written a short verse, in place of his missing photograph. As the astonished woman finished reading the inscriptions, her eyes filled with tears. For there, on the last page of the album, was a one hundred dollar bill that the rancher had slipped between the leaves.

· Thirteen ·

Christmas in
the Sod House
1864–1885

T he bitter winter wind howled around the rafters of the meager
sod house, and dust crept under the cracks of the doorframe and
single window, leaving a thin coating of dirt on the plank-board
dining table. The Suttons sat down before their open hearth to
celebrate the Christmastide. In place of the customary evergreen, the little
family had cut a scrawny cottonwood sapling from a nearby creek and
decorated its bare branches with pieces of tissue paper and cotton batting
from an old mattress.

The teenaged boy found a fine double-barreled shotgun under the
ignominious tree. His father received a much-needed saddle and a pair
of rugged leather gloves. The mother delighted in a new calico dress and
a set of fine china. On that Christmas morning on the bleak Dakota prairie,
the Suttons took needed time out from their never-ending chores to enjoy
their new Christmas presents—or at least vivid "pictures" of them. Like
many farm families of that generation on the far western plains, the
Suttons had cut illustrations of a shotgun, a saddle, gloves, a calico dress,
and a set of china from a well-weathered Montgomery Ward catalog and
placed them under the "Christmas tree."

The only "real gift" was a doily, knitted from a long rope of assorted
colored yarn. The only other treat was seed popcorn joyously prepared by
the entire family. Poverty, which was common among the homesteaders
on the sod house frontier, never precluded the celebration of Christmas

during the lean years. The scene was repeated from the windswept prairie lands of Montana to the edge of the desert in eastern New Mexico.

These hearty souls, who celebrated Christmas with almost no financial resources, eventually combined their determination for independence to conquer the West once and for all. Their numbers were astounding, considering their scant chances for success. In 1862 the U.S. Congress passed one of the most important pieces of legislation in U.S. history. The law, modestly known as the Homestead Act, bore witness to the belief that the West, principally the Great Plains, which rolled toward the Rocky Mountains, would be permanently settled in 160-acre allotments by pioneer farmers. The land was given free by the government to the farmer, who would live on it for five years and erect some sort of residence.

Historians have demonstrated that 160 acres were generally insufficient to obtain an adequate living from agriculture in that semiarid environment. In fact, cattlemen and land speculators benefited most from the Homestead Act and its subsequent amendments. But railroads, land agents, and even the western states and territories themselves beat the drums to attract settlers. They painted a picture of the western prairies as a Garden of Eden, watered by many streams and with flowering meadows stretching to the horizon.

In the western portion of the Great Plains, near the Rocky Mountains, the annual rainfall was usually inadequate to sustain the principal cereal crops. In addition, the velocity of the few streams meandering through the flat prairie lands was frequently too low to make irrigation practical, except very near the mountains. But farmers wanted to believe in the myth of the Garden of Eden, so they followed it into the West. Armed with farming tools and barbed wire, they came by the thousands during the last three decades of the nineteenth century. As a result, more people migrated west and more land was put under the plow between 1870 and 1890 than in all of America's past combined. By 1890 the frontier was gone forever.

Eternal optimism characterized these intrepid pioneer farmers. With free land and favorable prices for wheat, both in the United States and in Europe, how could they lose? Unfortunately for many, dreams and reality were far apart. Land agents failed to mention such catastrophes as drought, blizzards, and prairie fires. The necessity of obtaining more land and more equipment placed many a homesteader eternally in debt to the local bank or mortgage company. Railroads charged exorbitant rates for shipping and storing grain. Some homesteaders made it, some did not. At one time or another, almost all experienced indebtedness and poverty. The one time of the year, however, when the prairie farmer stopped to take account of himself and find needed respite was Christmastime. In the confines of a dark sod house or dugout in a hillside, the homesteader would celebrate the Yuletide as best he could.

As homestead claims were settled by farmers on the central plains, towns would quickly follow. Due to the permanent nature of agriculture, churches, schools, and businesses would shadow the farming frontier. As regions became more populated, farmers would lend aid to each other in times of strife, and at Christmas they shared their larder with neighbors. Witness the experiences of a young homesteader on the western Kansas prairies at Christmas, when a group of English immigrants to the plains combined their resources to make the Yuletide merry for their less-fortunate neighbors.

> One Christmas, I think of 1875, they [the Englishmen] thought to inject a little of good English Hallow-mass into the life of the prairies. So early that morning, they loaded up an old-fashioned sled with everything good to eat. A snow of four or five inches had fallen and the sledding was good. The load was all the team wanted to pull. With bells of all sizes and on all points of the harness, and men on top, they scurried over the prairies and dropped their Christmas greeting at the doors of the houses; a ham and a package of coffee at one place, a sack of corn-meal and a pound of tea at another, a turkey and some sugar at a third; and so on until the load was ended.

This idyllic scene, strongly reminiscent of Currier and Ives, became less frequent as the agricultural frontier passed the ninetieth meridian and spilled into western Nebraska, the Dakotas, eastern Colorado, Wyoming, and Montana, where the land was drier and neighbors farther apart. But despite the lonely prairie miles, neighbors still came to each other's aid in times of real need. One account tells of a destitute family on the bleak Dakota plains who had nothing for Christmas. The fair-haired daughter wished only for a little sister, and the small son also wanted a companion to play with. The children received their Christmas wishes when the mother gave birth to twins late on Christmas Eve. The only physician in the area had traveled over twenty miles by open sleigh in the midst of a wind-driven blizzard to tend the birthing. Surely no visit by St. Nicholas himself could have been more welcome in that desolate land.

During years when nature cooperated and the harvest was abundant, the larder stored in the family food cellar could produce legendary Christmas dinners. Toiling over an open hearth or a patented hay-burning stove with heavy iron skillets and Dutch ovens was the main Christmas Day activity for many a homesteading wife. Stuffed onions, mashed potatoes, homemade loaves of bread, and jellies made from wild plums or berries served as complements to main dishes of wild fowl, venison, or buffalo in earlier years. As eastern European, Scandinavian, and English immigrants obtained homesteads on the open plains, traditional Christmas recipes from their homelands were adapted to the plains, using existing fruits and vegetables grown in small gardens behind the sod house. English plum puddings were quite common on the prairie table, modified through the use of the versatile pumpkin, which grew abundantly in the sandy soil of the western plains. Many of "Grandma's" Christmas recipes, handed down to modern Christmas gourmands, in fact date from these early prairie adaptations.

As homesteaders further tamed the land and established towns and could afford to import lumber over the railroad, the sod houses were replaced by whitewashed frame structures. Perhaps a Christmas tree would come on the railroad, too, especially in later years. For those homesteaders who were fortunate enough to achieve stability on the land, Christmas celebrations commonly moved away from the home to community celebrations in the local church or the one-room schoolhouse. (Books were a rare commodity in the early prairie towns, so schools and churches usually took the initiative to accumulate small libraries. At Christmas, volumes of Dickens's *A Christmas Carol* or *Holly and Mistletoe* made the rounds among farm families.

In many cases, gifts were brought to the church for distribution on the Sunday before Christmas or during Christmas Eve services. Of course, schools would hold Christmas programs carefully planned by anxious classmates. Because children were a necessity on the frontier to help with the planting and the harvest, it was quite likely that school plays at Christmas attracted most of the adults in the community. Perhaps a cedar or bare cottonwood would be decorated with colored paper chains and strings of cranberries and popcorn and placed in a corner of the classroom. There might be a visit from Santa Claus, no matter how sparse his bag of gifts. (Most prairie St. Nicks were luckier than one in Plattsmouth, Nebraska, who backed into the burning candles on the school Christmas tree and caught his suit on fire.) School programs ended when desks and *McGuffie Readers* were shoved to the side of the room and the adults danced, while the boys chased the girls around the cedar floor, each boy intent on being the lucky fellow who pulled the most pigtails in a single evening.

Christmas on the prairie, in many ways, has not changed since its nineteenth-century origins. Schools and churches are still an important part of Yuletide, along with cherished family recipes. Neither has the economic condition of the family farmer changed significantly in many areas. Life is still hard. Children are still a necessity. Mortgages and low grain prices are still a harsh reality—a sad fate for the people who tamed the West and made it great. At Christmastime the plains farmer, like his pioneer ancestor, still stops, takes account of himself, and speculates nervously about what the new year might bring.

· Fourteen ·

St. Nicholas
on the Plains
1889

On the blustery, sage-covered prairie west of the one hundredth meridian, Christmas was often a day of bittersweet torment. Into that dry, harsh land of dust and snow that marks the western portions of the Dakotas and Nebraska and the eastern half of the old Wyoming Territory, came a few hearty farmers during the boom days of the 1880s. Unlike their brethren farther east in the so-called rain belt of the central plains, these pioneers discovered that mere survival in the arid heartland of the "Great American Desert" became an almost impossible ordeal. Tapping what few streams drained the Black Hills, the Big Horns, or the Medicine Bow mountains, these vigorous men and women were forced to construct and maintain a system of irrigation canals to bring life-giving water to their parched crops. During years of hardship, which were frequent in that land, Mother Nature tested the endurance of the pioneer spirit. Late frosts, blizzards, grasshopper plagues, and prairie fires could destroy hopes and dreams overnight.

At such times, the celebration of Christmas was a humble affair, devoid of the trappings and festivals that were by then commonplace in the little clapboard prairie towns to the east. With the closest neighbor sometimes a day's ride away, Christmas was a family occasion. Of course, Christmas trees were not to be found unless a homesteader lived adjacent to the mountains or high bluffs. Any gifts that were exchanged were made from the meager natural resources that were available. Christmas dinners were little more than what the family consumed on every other day of the year. The prospect of the new year evoked solemn moments of questioning, anxiety, and doubt as families huddled around cast-iron stoves, surrounded by a frozen wasteland.

Any community activities that existed at Christmastime were centered in small prairie churches. Because it was customary for homesteaders to donate a portion of strategically located land for a church, these symbols of permanence on the frontier sprang up early in newly settled regions. They became the first sites of community gatherings in the prairie states and territories and usually served double duty as a schoolhouse.

No permanent pastor served these humble houses of worship. The spiritual needs of frontier homesteaders were met by circuit riders. These stalwart frontier clergymen would spend the majority of their time traveling from one local church to the next, preaching interdenominational sermons, conducting weddings, performing baptisms, and comforting grieving families who had recently lost a loved one. Farmers on the frontier were fortunate indeed if their communities were visited once a month by a circuit rider. In times of hardship, the burden of keeping homesteaders' hopes and dreams alive fell to these noble men of the cloth.

Into this foreboding land at the base of Wyoming's Medicine Bow Range came a young circuit-riding missionary by the name of Cyrus Brady, fresh from the seminary in Omaha. It was Christmas Day 1889. Reverend Brady had been requested months in advance to perform a Christmas morning sermon at a little hillside church where Yuletide services had never before been held. After traveling to Cheyenne by Union Pacific express, Brady rented a two-horse sleigh for the final leg of the journey up-country to the small stone church, which sat high above the frozen banks of the Chugwater River.

As his sleigh moved swiftly across the bleak landscape, Brady reflected on the troubles that plains farmers had faced for the past couple of years. The summers had brought severe drought to the region. Streams had dried up. Crops had failed. Homesteaders had been forced to abandon their claims. Winters had been unusually harsh, with fierce blizzards hitting the northern plains. Driven by raging winds, the blowing snow and dust found its way into the snuggest of dwellings. It was impossible to keep the grit out of food cellars and living quarters. In December 1889 thirty-foot snowdrifts and temperatures lower than forty degrees below zero were not uncommon. Homesteaders would wake up in the morning to find food frozen on the table, jars of preserves broken in the pantry, and water turned to ice in the tea kettle. Wasting precious water for bathing was out of the question. Animals suffered more than humans. Ice had to be chipped away from the heads of cattle to keep them from smothering to death. Smaller animals could only survive indoors. Pioneer families found themselves living with hogs, chickens, calves, and even horses inside cramped sod houses for days on end, as the mercury hit new lows across the northern plains.

The giant cattle corporations had suffered since 1887. In some cases, 30 to 40 percent of their stock had been lost. The frozen, emaciated carcasses of the steers stacked up in draws and along barbed-wire fences, not to be discovered until the spring thaw. Brady shook his head and wondered how many people would be forced off the land before winter's end.

By early Christmas morning, Cyrus Brady had reached his destination. Upon entering the dilapidated little church, he noticed that a parishioner had built a fire in a "miserable, worn-out stove which hardly raised the temperature of the room a degree, although it filled the place with smoke." A cold wind penetrated the cracks in the church rafters. Little piles of snow formed on the altar. Only twelve people had braved the cold to attend the service that day. Brady conducted the short service wearing his father's tattered buffalo overcoat, a fur cap, and gloves. It was too bitter cold to wear his vestments.

After the service, Brady was invited to take Christmas dinner at the home of a nearby family, whose name is not known. The family's house consisted of a small combination dugout and stone dwelling, shored up with prairie sod. The floor was bare earth. Dirt was everywhere. During a recent thaw, melting snow had dripped a steady shower of muddy water through the roof, making it impossible to keep the home clean. The small, single room was dark and damp. It had the odor of moldy soil. There were two disheveled children, a little girl of six and a boy of five. Their clothes were ill-fitting, tattered, and dirty. Water to do laundry was not affordable. The impoverished family had no Christmas decorations. The meal itself was meager, consisting of their last cured ham. Brady noted:

> There was no turkey, and they did not even have a chicken. The menu was cornbread, ham and potatoes, and few potatoes at that. They were glad enough to get the ham. Their usual bill of fare was composed of potatoes and cornbread, and sometimes cornbread alone.

Brady's wife had packed a small mince pie for him before his journey. The children's eyes glistened as he produced the pie and divided it equally between the youngsters. "This pie makes it seem like Christmas, after all," said the little girl, with her mouth full.

"Yes," shouted the boy, "that and the ham."

"We didn't have any Christmas this year," continued the girl. "Last year mother made us some potato men" (little human figures made from potatoes and match sticks, with buttons for eyes).

"But this year," interrupted the boy, "potatoes are so scarce that we couldn't have 'em. Mother says that next year we might have some real Christmas."

The children were so brave that Brady's heart went out to them. He racked his brain for an idea to make their holiday a little brighter. Finally, something occurred to him.

After dinner, Brady excused himself and hurried back to the church. There he found two old baskets that were used for the collection. He selected the best one. Fortunately, Brady had in the pocket of his old buffalo coat a little sewing kit, which contained a pair of scissors, a thimble, stitching needles, thread, a small pincushion, an emery bag, and a variety of buttons. He emptied the contents of the sewing kit into the collection basket and decorated it with bright ribbon ties, ripped off the leather bag that had held his sewing supplies. Satisfied with his creation, the clergyman went back to the house.

To the boy he gave his new penknife and to the girl he presented the church basket with the sewing things neatly arranged inside. The children were ecstatic. The brave little folks had stoically resolved themselves to having no Christmas. All they had to look forward to was a long winter of suffering and perhaps hunger. Tears came to Brady's eyes. During his long journey home he recorded the exact moment in his journal.

> The joy of those children was one of the finest things I have ever witnessed. The face of the little girl was positively filled with awe as she lifted from the basket, one by one, the pretty and useful articles, and when I added a small box of candy that my children had provided me, they looked at me with feelings of reverence, almost as a visible incarnation of Santa Claus. They were the cheapest and most effective Christmas presents it was ever my pleasure to bestow. I hope to be forgiven for putting the church furniture to such a secular use.

It is perhaps difficult in this modern age of high expectation to fully comprehend how such a simple act of charity as this could bring such boundless joy. But before his departure, the grateful family told the clergyman that he had renewed their hope for the future. They would try to stay on the land and make a go of their farm. History does not record whether they succeeded. But during that year, the northern plains were hit with a late spring blizzard, one of the biggest in recent memory. Farmers were ruined. The open-range cattle industry had all but come to an end as foreign investors pulled out of the business.

Of all the homestead claims filed on the northern plains between 1885 and 1890, final patents in some regions were issued to less than 30 percent of the homesteaders by the end of the required residency period. When conditions were hard, as they were in the late 1880s, homesteaders became discouraged. This dejection was especially felt at Christmas. During the Yuletide season, pioneers quite naturally sought and received signs of encouragement from the pastors moving among their little churches dotting the prairie. Today, the fields of waving grain that extend from horizon to horizon in parts of southeastern Wyoming stand as a testament to the ultimate success of the ministers' faith and the innovation of pioneers living in that harsh land. We will never know how many brave farmers would have given up if it were not for the efforts of the unheralded itinerant clergymen, who moved through the frontier offering hope and occasionally, at Christmas, even assuming the identity of St. Nicholas on the plains.

The life of a soldier on the western

frontier was harsh and often brutal,

particularly in the winter.

Denver Public Library,

Western History Department

· Fifteen ·

A Soldier's Christmas
1868–1890

I f you were a soldier on the western plains, your toast to Christmas might be, Eat, drink, and be merry, for tomorrow we die!

Not a good excuse, but it has been sufficient on many occasions to be true. The soldier on campaign passes life easily. He holds it in no strong grip, and the Merry Christmas evening is as liable to be spent in the saddle in fierce combat with the blizzard as in his cozy tepee with his comrades and his scant cheer. The jug containing the spirits of the occasion may have been gotten from a town fifty miles away on the railroad.

It is never a late evening, such a one as this, it's just a few stolen moments from the "demnition grind." The last arrival may be a youngster just in from patrol, who explains that he just "cut the trail of forty or fifty Sioux five miles below, on the crossing of the White River"; and you may hear the bugle, and the bugle may blow quick and often, and if the bugle does mingle its notes with the howling of the blizzard, you will discover that the occasion is not one of merriment. But let us hope that it will not blow.

The words are those of the renowned western illustrator and correspondent, Frederic Remington, who knew the pony soldier as well as anyone. And his description of a soldier's Christmas Eve on the frozen Dakota prairie epitomizes the solitude and malaise experienced by countless men of the ranks at Christmastide during the bloody Indian wars.

Between 1864 and 1890, as the great agricultural frontier swept westward across the plains to the very threshold of the Rocky Mountains, the native inhabitants of the land saw the determination of the pioneer farmer to fence the ranges, break the sod, and alter the landscape forever. The movement, which destroyed the expansive buffalo ranges, spelled doom for the Plains Indian—and he fought back for his very survival. Against the greatest light cavalry in the world, the white man's "Great Soldier Chief" in Washington hurled a never-ending procession of blue-clad volunteers to track the Indian to the heart of his mother country and then to relocate him on alien soil.

Contrary to the romantic impression, the years between 1865 and 1898 witnessed a low ebb in the professional quality of the regular United States Army. A nation healing its wounds from the devastation of a bloody civil war turned inward and longed for peace and isolation. The army, faced with clearing the western plains for settlement, consequently attracted a questionable element into its ranks. Drifters, malcontents, ex-Confederate veterans who had lost property during the war, irreconcilable bigots bent on the total genocide of the red race, even wanted men seeking refuge from the law composed an alarming proportion of the enlisted ranks—along with a few very able career soldiers. Meager rations, low pay, and long, grinding days in the saddle characterized their monotonous existence.

Christmas Eve might find them on campaign, spending the holiday by lantern light in a bone-chilling Sibley tent, as Remington described, buttoned up to their chins in huge canvas overcoats and muskrat caps. Resigned to the fact that, for them, life's pleasures usually comprised little more than a good smoke and a big belt of cheap whiskey, they commonly celebrated Christmas deep in their cups.

Such was the case for the men of the Seventh Cavalry over Christmas 1868. During that bleak year on the southern plains, General Philip Sheridan, disgusted by his failure to subjugate the Cheyenne during their raids of revenge, which were in response to the infamous Sand Creek Massacre in Colorado Territory four years before, inaugurated a grand winter campaign to strike terror in the red men's camps hidden away in the old Indian Territory that became Oklahoma. Led by the dashing Lieutenant Colonel George Armstrong Custer, the Seventh was successful in smashing the unsuspecting camp of Chief Black Kettle along the banks of the Washita River in the early morning of November 27.

Moving downriver after the battle, the Seventh could be found at Christmas camped in the vicinity of old Fort Cobb. A private in the regiment recalled how a cold wind on Christmas Day forced the men into their tents, where they spent the afternoon gambling and drinking "so the brightness [of the day] would not be wasted."

More often, however, the wearisome winter months would be spent quartered within the confines of one of the many western military posts. With nothing to do but drill and tend his horse, the soldier's life became one of intense boredom. In the musty barracks or dark stables, amidst the aroma of stale hay and saddle soap, card games and hard drinking would constitute his pitiful recreation. The situation was not altered much by the advent of Christmas. Regimental get-togethers might be held, but more often whiskey ration vouchers, which had been held back during the autumn months, were distributed to the men on Christmas Eve. The sutler's saloon would then become a scene of unmitigated clamor as enlisted men would exhaust the Yuletide sitting at the poker tables or standing at a burnished oak bar.

Army life in the West was a little brighter for the officer corps, even though they were confined to the same isolated environment as enlisted men. On the whole, professional officers after the Civil War were dedicated to their work, and their relative competence exceeded that of the enlisted ranks. In numerous cases, officers would bring their wives and children to live with them in private quarters provided at the western outposts. The life of an army wife was lonely, monotonous, and anxious during times when her husband was out on patrol. Nevertheless, the highlight of the year for these women and their husbands was Christmastime. Gala parties were frequently held, and relatives from the East might visit their military families for the holidays.

During one cold Christmas season in the 1860s, Catharine Wever Collins left Hillsboro, Ohio, to join her husband, Colonel William O. Collins, then commanding the Eleventh Ohio Volunteer Cavalry, and her son, Lieutenant Caspar W. Collins, at Fort Laramie, Wyoming Territory. After attending a Christmas dinner given by the officers of Company D on Christmas night, Mrs. Collins noted:

> They had roast pig, roast beef and boiled ham, jellies, pickles, coffee, tea, peaches, cake, mince pie and ice cream. The tables looked very handsomely. I cannot think where they got all their table cloths and dishes, but everything was arranged with taste and judgement. A large cake, nicely iced and a basket of flowers on it with the inscription Co. D, 11th Cav. in large raised letters was much admired.

Mrs. Collins observed that the host officer's house was "beautiful though not large with handsome curtains to the 3 windows, a beautiful Brussels carpet, a few pictures and other nice furniture." In one corner of the small parlor were two crystal bowls filled with eggnog and served in cut-crystal goblets. A few military campaign songs were sung after supper and toasts were made to the good fortune of the regiment.

Mrs. Collins could not know on that crisp Christmas night at Fort Laramie that in a very short time a budding young city in Colorado Territory would bear her husband's name—Fort Collins—and that a major city in Wyoming would be named Caspar in tribute to her son, who died attempting to rescue a beleaguered supply train from an attack by the Indians.

The fine food and drink enjoyed by officers and their wives at Christmas came on the railroad and was then hauled to the isolated military outposts by those workhorses of the prairies, the western freighters. Fancy presents from the East also came on the railroads. Officers' children would hang their stockings on December 24 like any children anywhere in America. Snuggled under a bulky buffalo-hide blanket, in a huge cast-iron army bed upstairs in a wood-frame army house, with the moonlight reflecting off the prairie snow through thickly paned army windows, they would anxiously await the arrival of Santa Claus. The jolly elfin figure of Santa Claus was just becoming popularized in the 1860s through the illustrations of political cartoonist Thomas Nast in a national magazine frequently read by the army, *Harper's Weekly*. On Christmas morning, the children would trundle downstairs to find ornate Victorian rocking horses or chubby-cheeked dolls dressed in quaint lace nightgowns. After glowing over their treasures, they would perhaps miss their fathers, who were out on patrol in the teeth of a prairie storm.

When families were together on Christmas Day, the bustling activities of garrison life paralleled any Christmas festivities anywhere in the West. Mrs. Elizabeth Bacon Custer, who accompanied her flamboyant husband to several isolated military outposts on the Great Plains, always looked forward with much excitement to the joyous season. In one of her unpublished manuscripts, which lay undiscovered until the 1960s, Mrs. Custer described those Christmas days spent on the plains with her devoted "Autie" and their friends.

> One universal custom was for all of us to spend all the time we could together. All day long the officers were running in and out of every door, the "wish you Merry Christmas" rang out over the parade ground after any man who was crossing to attend to some duty and had not shown up among us. We usually had a sleigh ride and everyone sang and laughed as we sped over the country where there were no neighbors to be disturbed by our gaiety. If it was warm enough there poured out of the garrison a cavalcade vehemently talking, gesticulating, laughing or humming bars of Christmas carols remembered from childhood, or starting some wild or convivial chorus where everybody announced that they "wouldn't go home till morning" in notes very emphatic if not entirely musical.

> Later in the evening, when the music came up from the band quarters, we all went to the house of the commanding officer to dance.

> With a garrison full of perfectly healthful people with a determination to be merry, notwithstanding the isolated life and utterly dreary surroundings, the holidays were made something to look forward to the whole year round.

Golden moments such as these had to be treasured with much love by officers' wives because they never knew when they might end. Beginning in 1876, Libby Custer spent nearly fifty-seven years in widowhood, after her husband, along with five companies of his famed Seventh Cavalry, were annihilated by Crazy Horse's warriors on the somber bluffs above the Montana stream that the Sioux called the Greasy Grass and the white man called the Little Big Horn.

Of course, the luckless trooper dreaded being engaged in mortal combat during the Christmas holidays. On Christmas Eve 1890, "Boots and Saddles" sounded on the desolate South Dakota prairie for the men of the Sixth Cavalry. Their orders were to apprehend a large band of recalcitrant Sioux Ghost Dancers under Chief Big Foot near the White River. Confined to the reservation, the proud but defeated Sioux had witnessed the slow and methodical dissolution of their old ways at the hands of the white man's well-meaning but unenlightened reformers. For well over a decade, they had been indigent wards of the bereft Pine Ridge Agency. Facing the final extinction of their culture, the Sioux reacted in a manner common to crumbling civilizations—they placed their last hopes in the coming of a messiah. His name was Wovoka, an old Paiute medicine man who came among the Sioux in 1889 preaching the gospel of the Ghost Dance. By performing the long, trancelike dance, it was believed that the ghosts of Indians long dead would be resurrected to drive out the white intruders, bring back the buffalo, and restore the old way of life.

The army became alarmed by the dances, which were most avidly practiced by Big Foot's band, and they took steps to suppress them. Among these efforts was the December 24 patrol of Colonel Eugene Asa Carr's Sixth Cavalry. In the evening the column camped on the banks of Sage Creek, near the edge of the foreboding Dakota badlands. In those eerie surroundings, the troopers of the Sixth Cavalry spent a cheerless Christmas Eve trying to sleep under their thin saddle blankets.

By December 26 the Seventh Cavalry, under Colonel James W. Forsythe, was also in the field with orders to disarm the Ghost Dancers. Three days later, after locating the group of between 250 and 350 Sioux, mostly old men and women, a disturbance began when troopers of the Seventh attempted to search the Indians for weapons. Reportedly a shot was fired from the Indian side—and the slaughter began. The millennium predicted by the Ghost Dance messiah did not come. In its place were four rapid-firing Hotchkiss field artillery pieces that rained death on more than half of Big Foot's sickened people.

This tragic and unnecessary event brought an end to the long struggle for Indian self-assertion during the nineteenth century. It is highly ironic that the hopeful promise of the Sioux messiah met such a final and violent end at the very season of the year when the white people were celebrating the birth of another messiah in a humble manger almost two thousand years ago—a messiah whose promise of "peace on earth, goodwill toward men" was left unfulfilled that Christmas in 1890 in the blood-splattered snows of Wounded Knee.

If you were a soldier on the western plains, you might ponder your mortality as you head for your Sibley tent, another Christmas gone. "You stumble through snow-laden willows and face the cutting blast, while the clash and 'Halt!' of the sentinel stops you here and there. You pull off your boots and crawl into your blankets quickly before the infernal Sibley stove gives its sigh as the last departing spark goes up the chimney, and leaves the winds and drifting snows to bellow and scream over the wild wastes."

· Sixteen ·

Christmas Eve
in San Felipé
Early 1900s

N estled in the heart of the upper Rio Grande Valley, between Albuquerque and Santa Fe, stands the enigmatic pueblo of San Felipé. Its time-weathered adobes and ancient plaza plunge the uninitiated Christmas wayfarer into a timeless world of mystical tranquility. One of about twenty remaining dwellings of the proud Puebloan cultures of the Southwest, which trace their cultural origins to a time long before the coming of the Europeans, San Felipé and its neighboring communities entered the twentieth century as stolid relics of past glory — vestiges of endurance in an age of intolerance and technological alteration of nature itself. Taos, Isleta, Santa Domingo, Acoma (the Sky City), Santa Clara, Tesuque, and others — their names are legendary in the southern Rockies.

These communities rose from the visions of the Anasazi, the ancient ones of the Colorado Plateau, who concentrated their agricultural societies along the Rio Grande sometime after A.D. 1300. They endured the punishing Spanish conquest, colonial revolution, war, and the march of U.S. civilization. No one knows the reason for the migration of Puebloan peoples to the Rio Grande. Perhaps famine, pressure from plundering Apaches and Navajos, epidemic, or internal discord caused the movement of these ingenious societies to the fertile valley of the great river. Undoubtedly their dwellings were mistaken for the legendary Cities of Cibola. When viewed from great distances by the early Spanish explorers Nunez

Cabeza de Vaca and Friar Marcos de Niza, their sunbaked walls, when reflected by the setting sun through the mirage-like heat vapors of the parched desert, indeed appeared to be made of gold.

Long neglected save for the proselytizing endeavors of the zealous Franciscan priests, the ancient cities were "rediscovered" about the turn of the twentieth century by romantic Americans.

The pioneer painters of the Taos Society of Artists, who came to the Rockies' southern chain in the early twentieth century to capture the pastel hues of sky, mountain, and sun-bleached land, found more suitable subjects among the native inhabitants of the piñon bluffs and high plateaus. Walter Ufer, Joseph Henry Sharp, Irving Crouse, Bert Phillips, Ernest Blumenschein, and others entered the Southwest at the end of the frontier period. Collectively these frontier artists' expressionistic canvases reveal the timelessness of the land and its people, as well as ancient tradition, ceremony, and cultural history.

Cautious not to violate the sanctity of religious practice through the invasion of camera or notebook, some of these painters haunted the back roads of northern New Mexico, visiting the people and observing colorful rituals. What they found was a unique social system steeped in tradition but modified by contact with a diversity of colorful cultures. A religion based on the concept of living in harmony with nature, they discovered, transcends all else but has assimilated without conflict the practices of Spain, Mexico, and the United States into its complex scheme. Nominally Christianized by the Spanish, the Puebloan people integrated the glorification of patron saints into their rituals. They honor the Yuletide season in the same fashion that early Christians melded the birth of their savior with the winter solstice. With the exception of the colorful Penitente rituals during Holy Week, the Christmas season offered perhaps the most rewarding time of the year for Taos artists to prowl the region's ancient communities for renewal and inspiration—and it still does. Perhaps in no other locale on earth can the visitor still witness age-old traditions of Yuletide, from Christmas Eve through the Epiphany, mostly unchanged.

Late on Christmas Eve, an artist might leave the warmth of the Christmas hearth to travel by rickety buckboard the pitch-dark, snow-dusted back roads of the New Mexican highlands. One year it might be Taos Pueblo or San Felipé, the next Isleta or Laguna—it did not matter. Such decisions were left to the inspiration of the season rather than to prior planning. After locating the burnt ocher walls of the eroded pueblo, he might hurry with frosty breath to the Franciscan church built on so many years ago by dedicated evangelists in the wilderness. Pushing open a creaking, worm-eaten wood door, the Christmas wanderer would walk across the packed adobe floor and make his way toward a grotesque iron stove faintly glowing red in the corner of the cold, dark sanctuary. There would be no benches in the church, and the visitor would have to content himself with leaning against a damp earthen wall amidst other shadowy spectators. A few candles in tin holders would provide faint illumination for the dank sanctuary. There the artist would wait in silence, seemingly forever.

But across the well-worn plaza, where generations have trod, an ancient ritual is about to take place, as dark figures descend a twisted and weathered cedar wood ladder into the depths of an age-old kiva. A small fire has been started in the kiva. The pungent aroma of wood smoke ascends to the top of the subterranean chamber and floats across the plaza to moisten the eyes of heavily blanketed figures silently scurrying through the blackness toward the ancient church. Inside the chamber, the light from the fire flickers irregularly and subtly illuminates eerie, distorted human images against the underground walls. Strange costumes of fur and buckskin are being donned with austere reverence. Once the figures leave the underground cavern, their profiles will remind any tardy visitors of ancient Druid worshipers on England's Salisbury Plain, centuries back in time.

Finally, the congregation inside the cold church hears the faint, muffled "thump" of animal-skin drums as the procession leaves the kiva and makes its way to the sanctuary. Very slowly the rawhide drumbeats grow louder. The doors swing open, and a line of dark figures enter, eight abreast. The distinct rhythm of the drums stirs a chill along the spines of the congregation. About forty men slowly bob and weave around the drums. Faint chanting begins, growing louder as the ceremony continues. Gourd rattles keep the rhythm of the drums perfectly. The drums do not stop but grow louder almost imperceptibly. The mind of the Anglo artist becomes confused at the sight of such a pagan ritual being methodically acted out inside a Christian church. The chanters, however, perceive no incongruity. Since the beginning of the world, this has been a time for dancing—a time to honor the solstice, to speed the year on its way toward the return of the sun.

After the drone of the drums has mesmerized the congregation, there suddenly appears a burst of light as a hundred candles are simultaneously lit and placed on the once-blackened altar. The celebrants drop to their knees, and a young Hispanic priest enters the room behind the altar. For the next hour, the midnight Mass is performed in perfect Latin. The interweaving of ancient cultures has been played out once again, as it has been for centuries.

Toward the morning of Christmas Day, the congregation silently leaves. The artist in their midst knows that tomorrow he must paint. He knows that he must try to capture the mystery and the irony of those past moments on Christmas Eve. But deep down in his heart, he knows that he will not fully succeed. The traditions are too mysterious, too ancient, too perfect—and he is among the uninitiated and will always remain so. Quietly he returns home, his buckboard rattling along on deserted, snow-dusted roads. He is refreshed by the early-Christmas-morning scent of desert creosote penetrating the dry air of another timeless New Mexican dawn.

Part Four

FROM
WILDERNESS
TO
CIVILIZATION

· Seventeen ·

Christmastime in the City
An Old-World Medley
1871–1892

Nowhere in the Rocky Mountain West did the rich variety of Christmas traditions find such ready acceptance as in the cities. As early as the 1870s, the principal urban centers of the Rockies were well on their way to developing an air of urbane sophistication and refinement. After the initial years of trial, Salt Lake City had grown up to become the "Gem of the Rockies." As more and more of the faithful tramped the plains to the New Zion, the rich traditions introduced by Brigham Young spread and became permanent fixtures of the Mormon Christmas. In Santa Fe and Albuquerque, Anglo-American traditions had thoroughly merged with Hispanic and Native American rituals and festivals by 1870. New Mexico became a veritable showcase for multiethnic Christmas celebrations. But in no other place did western European customs find such a ready welcome at Yuletide than in the homes of the more affluent in the Queen City of the Plains—Denver.

In comparison to eastern metropolises, Denver retained much of her wide-open frontier character in 1870. Nevertheless, she had grown up considerably from her uncertain beginnings along the dusty banks of Cherry Creek. After a devastating fire in 1863 and an equally ravaging flood the following year, the city was rebuilt almost entirely of brick. Business flourished after railroad connections were completed in 1870. As chief supplier of the mines to the west, Denver became the principal service center for the eastern slope of the Rocky Mountain empire. This relative prosperity attracted stable families to the city, and many affluent immigrants who found opportunity in the young metropolis after 1870 were Western Europeans.

As Denver's boosters sought means to develop the economy of the city, they attracted foreign capital to the region. A substantial proportion of the entrepreneurs who invested in the economy of the Rocky Mountain region were from the British Isles. As their profits rolled in from railroad freighting, the mines at Leadville, and the open-range cattle industry, many of these British investors moved to Denver. There they built hotels, office buildings, and splendid homes. They also brought rich old-world traditions of Christmas to the Rocky Mountain region. As these wealthy British investors gained access to Denver's prosperous social circles, they introduced their U.S.-born neighbors to the Yuletide pleasures they had cherished in their homeland and in turn became enthralled with the simple frontier customs of a "Yankee Christmas." From the beginning of the decade of the 1870s, many British subjects visited their relatives and friends in the "Wild West" at Christmastime. In this fashion they kept British practices alive in Denver, while taking back to England or Scotland customs born of the western frontier. The result was a blending of Christmas traditions on both sides of the ocean.

One of the earliest records of Christmastide in growing Denver was written by Rose Georgina Kingsley, an upper-class Englishwoman and daughter of the internationally famous British novelist Charles Kingsley. Arriving in the city to visit a friend just before Christmas in 1871, Kingsley became enchanted with the holiday activity surrounding her. As was customary among cultured women of the Victorian era, she kept a meticulous diary. Entering the city by stagecoach, she reported that

> Denver looks wintry enough, under six inches to a foot of snow: but it is full of life and bustle. The toy-shops are gay with preparations of Christmas-trees; the candy stores filled with the most attractive sweetmeats; the furriers display beaver coats, and mink, ermine, and sable, to tempt the cold passer-by; and in the butchers' shops hang, besides the ordinary beef and mutton, buffalo, blacked-tailed deer, antelope, Rocky Mountain sheep, quails, partridges, and prairie-chicken.

Moving uptown from the commercial center along Blake Street, Rose Kingsley entered the affluent residential section of frontier Denver situated along Fourteenth Street, past Larimer. There she noticed:

> The streets are full of sleighs, each horse with its collar of bells; and all the little boys have manufactured or bought little sleds, which they tie to the back of any passing cart or carriage; and get whisked along the streets till some sharp turn or unusual roughness in the road upsets them.

Strolling through the city with three friends, Rose discovered that the crude board sidewalks that bordered the unpaved streets ended abruptly at alleyways and in front of vacant lots, creating "a corresponding gap" along the street. Because the bustling avenues were covererd with snow, her friends did not see one of the hidden precipices and walked calmly over the end of the sidewalk, which was elevated nearly two feet above the street. All three fell "flat in the snow side by side," petticoats and pantalettes fuly displayed beneath their hooped skirts "much to the delight of the passers-by." Despite such hazards, Rose Kingsley fell in love with Denver and noted that "in the frank and unconventional state of society which exists in the West, friendships are made much more easily than even in the Eastern States, or still more, in our English society."

Although the recent snowfall had "spoiled the ice for skating," what better time than Christmas Eve to go for a sleigh ride? Rose and her male companion were bundled up in "blankets and buffalo robes and all their sable furs," for the thermometer stood at two degrees below zero. The freshly tanned buffalo robes were warm but smelled "musty," even in the out-of-doors. As the open sleigh left the city behind, under the bright moonlight of the open prairie, Rose Kingsley could see the frozen breath of the horses as they flew over the smooth, sparkling snow, with bells "jingling in the frosty air." When they arrived home, about 11:00 P.M., Rose noted that her companion "looked just like Santa Claus, with his moustache and hair all snowy white from his frozen breath."

Christmas Day dawned bright, and Rose had to pick her way through rivers of melting snow on her way to St. John's Episcopal Church, located then at the corner of Fourteenth and Arapahoe streets. Devoted to the established Church of England, many British-born Denver residents attended services at the little Episcopal church that reminded Rose of a "coach-house" on the outside. Inside, however, the altars were tastefully decorated with fresh evergreens from the mountains.

After church services, the Englishwoman was invited to eat Christmas dinner at the home of a well-to-do friend who lived in the fashionable residential area of the city. The meal consisted of orthodox "turkey and mince-pie." Afterward the guests were summoned to the spacious drawing room, where a fresh spruce tree had been decorated with "strings of raw cranberries and snowy popcorn." After presents were distributed to the household servants, the guests settled down to an evening of singing and parlor games—an old English tradition on Christmas. It is possible that Rose Kingsley introduced the American guests to the Dickensian games of blindman's buff, charades, or the most popular of Victorian parlor amusements at Christmastime—snapdragon. In the latter game, a shallow bowl was filled with spirits and currants and placed on the floor. The liquor was ignited. Players then attempted to grab a currant out of the flames and put it into their mouths. The idea was to close the mouth over the burning currant quickly and extinguish the flame before any of the opponents could do so.

As the evening drew to a close, Rose treated the American guests to a taste of flaming English plum pudding, which she had prepared the week before. Although no respectable Briton would be without his "pudding" at Christmas, many of the American guests found the brandy-laden flambé bland and tasteless. The evening came to a glorious end with the guests, both English and American, toasting the new year and singing "God Save the Queen."

By the 1880s, the Denver Rose Kingsley had known was gone. Silver had become the magnet that attracted even more investment into the city from the British Isles. The affluent residential area of the city moved from Fourteenth Street to the plateau around the new state capitol grounds. In that neighborhood, Colorado's silver kings and cattle barons built massive stone mansions to showcase their newfound wealth. Streets were paved, yards were seeded and irrigated from a city canal, and Denver's elite, both American and European, lived their lives in opulent splendor, secluded from the working classes located in older sections of town.

One of this elite in 1880 was an industrious Scot by the name of James Duff. Not wishing to oversee his railroad investments from Scotland, Duff moved to Denver, where he poured money into rail networks, the cattle business, Leadville silver mines, real estate, and irrigation projects. He built the Barclay Block in the expanding business district of the young city. He also built the plush Windsor Hotel at the corner of Eighteenth and Larimer streets. Without a doubt, the Windsor was the finest hostelry in the Rocky Mountain West when it first opened its doors on June 23, 1880. Duff engaged an English corporation to build the palatial hotel for a sum exceeding $650,000. Its lobby featured skylights, a solid walnut staircase, and a gas-jetted chandelier. The stone was hauled in from Castle Rock, thirty miles south of Denver. Famous from New York to San Francisco, the Windsor catered to the elite. Oscar Wilde, Robert Louis Stevenson, George Bernard Shaw—and of course the eccentric editor of the *Denver Tribune,* Eugene Field—all frequented the plush saloons of the Windsor, where they would swap poems for shots of imported whiskey. Although the hotel was leased shortly before completion to a group of local businessmen, including Maxcy Tabor, the son of silver magnate Horace W. Tabor, for the next decade, James Duff and others like him threw some of the most lavish parties in the history of the Rocky Mountain region at the Windsor—some of them at Christmastime.

The guest lists for these parties included the upper crust of Denver society. They also included wealthy Europeans who relished a touch of civilization halfway around the world. The price of admission was high. But at Christmas the gentry of the Rocky Mountains dined in extravagant luxury. The Windsor's manager, William Bush, engaged a staff of thirty-two waiters, imported from Chicago. He set the tables with fine linen, Reed and Barton silver, gold-rimmed Haviland china, and sparkling crystal goblets. The hotel imported oysters from the East, exotic guava jelly, and wild game freshly shot in the mountains by commissioned hunters. In addition to local delicacies, guests were introduced to the traditional Boar's Head feast, an old English Christmas tradition dating back to the Middle Ages and kept alive by Queen Victoria herself at Windsor Castle. The head of an imported wild boar was cleaned and cooked in Madeira, along with an unending assortment of seasonings. When done, the tusked main dish was hoisted on a golden litter and ceremoniously carried into the dining room by four waiters appropriately dressed in sixteenth-century costume. A large portion of the proceeds of these Christmas balls went to charity. In fact, profits from the Windsor's social season actually kept little St. Luke's Hospital in neighboring Highlands alive during the 1880s.

Not all of the Western European *haut monde* who found their way to Denver during the late nineteenth century were of British extraction. Indeed, a substantial proportion of Denver's early population was German. Four miles east of Broadway, outside Denver's city limits in 1889, was the idyllic suburb of Montclair. Designed to be a haven from city bustle for affluent Denverites, the community was basically the brainstorm of Baron Walter von Richthofen, a red-bearded German nobleman from the famous clan that would one day include the celebrated Red Baron, Manfred von Richthofen, flying ace of Germany during World War I.

Walter von Richthofen was born in Kriesenitz, Silesia, in 1848, a broad agricultural belt in Germany not unlike the plains of eastern Colorado. He served as an officer in the Franco-Prussian War of 1870–1871. During the late 1870s, Richthofen went to New York and shortly afterward to Colorado. After viewing the shining mountains and the enormous potential ahead for booming Denver, he decided to settle permanently in the Queen City. It is believed that he tried his hand at cattle ranching for a time after his arrival and failed. After several unsuccessful real estate ventures and numerous other development schemes, the flamboyant and dashing Richthofen decided that the prairie east of the city was ripe for exploitation and development. He envisioned an elite suburb—green, tree lined, and peaceful—away from urban noise and bustle.

To this end, the baron acquired most of the land that was to become Montclair. On it he built a resplendent medieval castle from quarried stone, complete with a moat, an emblazoned coat of arms, and a stone effigy of the legendary Teutonic King Barbarossa. He brought in irrigation water and planted box elder trees and spruce from Bear Creek Canyon to the west. Around his castle he fenced in several acres where deer and antelope were kept. He even built a bear pit for his amusement. Into the blue skies above Montclair, Richthofen released a flock of hardy canaries to grace the trees and shrubs in the quiet neighborhood. Soon ornate tallyho coaches

were seen entering the suburb, escorted by the baron himself and his Russian wolfhounds, dashing ahead of the coaches filled with potential land buyers. Eventually a few respectable homes popped up around the conspicuous castle. It seemed that Montclair would become a success.

In 1887 the red-bearded baron married for the second time. The new baroness was a lovely Englishwoman by the name of Louise Ferguson Davies. Like Richthofen himself, she had been divorced. By 1889 she was living with her husband at the castle. The new Mrs. Richthofen was never fully accepted by Denver's snobbish society matrons. She was, after all, a divorcée. Perhaps worse, she went to the extreme of actually dying her hair! She was always lonely at Montclair. Although neighbors generally shunned the eccentric Richthofens, the children of the community were always welcome at the extravagant parties held for them at the castle. The most lavish of these parties were given at Christmastime, when traditional German customs were richly displayed.

As the American children entered the foyer of the spacious estate, they saw the huge Colorado blue spruce, freshly cut in the mountains. The tree was profusely decorated with delicate, handblown glass ornaments representing snowmen, cherubs, and exotic birds. The baron imported these treasures from cottage artisans residing in the picturesque German village of Lauscha, high in the forested Thuringian mountains. Delicate oil lamps would be lit on the tree for the children's pleasure. Perhaps there would be a visit from the *Weihnachtsmann,* Father Christmas, the Prussian equivalent of Santa Claus. Small gifts and confections would be distributed by this white-bearded figure with much fanfare and to the extreme consternation of the nervous wolfhounds trying to nap by the fireplace.

Because Germans celebrated all twelve days of Christmas, the parties at the Richthofen castle were numerous during Christmas week. As the boys amused themselves at the bear pit, little girls in linen dresses and calico aprons would be found in the kitchen with Mrs. Richthofen and her household staff preparing elaborately decorated Black Forest cakes, marzipan, and gingerbreads. The old German carol "Stille Nacht, Heilige Nacht" ("Silent Night") might be sung as the sun set over Long's Peak. On mild evenings, the children would be led along the streets of Montclair, knocking on doors and tossing small anonymous gifts into the hallways of homes as servants or masters of the house answered their doors. Many times hot chocolate and other treats were offered to the children practicing this newly learned tradition of the *Klopfelscheitt,* a German version of the English-inspired caroling ensembles tramping the streets of Capitol Hill on the same evenings.

Ultimately, Baron von Richthofen's dream of creating a genteel community in the pioneer suburb of Montclair failed like his other elaborate schemes. He left the castle after only three years and died in Denver's

Hotel L'Imperiale on May 8, 1898, following an appendectomy. No longer do stately wolfhounds herald the arrival of the *Weihnachtsmann*.

Horse-drawn sleighs no longer fly silently on silken snow across the prairie east of town. And the once-elegant Windsor Hotel was razed in 1959 to make way for a parking lot. But the old-world traditions of Christmas are still present in Denver. European delicacies, plum puddings, and Black Forest cakes may still be purchased in pastry shops throughout the community. The German and English versions of St. Nicholas and Father Christmas have blended well with the concept of Santa Claus. European carols are sung in churches and on the bustling streets of Larimer Square every Christmas season. The Teutonic tradition of decorating evergreen trees is taken for granted.

The elite of western European society came to Denver during the waning years of the nineteenth century. Aside from the desire to compile fortunes, these Europeans had the common bond of bringing refinement to the frontier city. To a degree they succeeded and, in return, absorbed elements of frontier romanticism into their own lives and culture. Today their beloved Christmas customs are imperceptibly integrated into the celebration of Christmas, along with native customs inherited from the mountain man, the Basque shepherd of the Southwest, and the Native American.

Christmas, circa 1900.

Colorado Historical Society

· Eighteen ·

Christmas Trees
1865–1914

T he tradition of decorating fresh evergreen trees at Christmastime is the most widespread Yuletide custom in the United States today. Surprisingly, however, there is scant mention of Christmas trees in the diaries and accounts of U.S. citizens prior to 1850. Unquestionably, the tradition originated in the Bavarian forests of Germany and first made its way to the United States with Teutonic immigrants settling in Pennsylvania. As Germans moved west along the successive frontiers of the expanding nation, the Christmas tree moved with them. The Germans were one of the largest immigrant groups to settle in the West, and they popularized Christmas trees among their neighbors along the frontier. Consequently, the institution caught on more rapidly in the West than it had during the years required to settle the lands east of the Mississippi River.

The custom was further reinforced when Prince Albert of Saxe-Coburg, the Prussian spouse of Queen Victoria, popularized German Christmas trees in Great Britain after 1841. Due to the general esteem Americans felt for Queen Victoria and the large numbers of British immigrants to the West, the Christmas tree became even more popular after the passage of the Homestead Act in 1862. Following that year, a host of homesteaders, some of whom were of English and German extraction, took advantage of the opportunity to obtain free government land, and they brought the tradition of the Christmas tree with them to their new homes. Despite the seemingly rapid spread of the tradition of decorating evergreen trees, the custom did not gain wide acceptance in the United States and the West until the last two or three decades of the nineteenth century.

Of course, the pioneers who settled in or near the Rockies found a never-ending abundance of pine and spruce growing on the slopes of the great peaks and in the foothills. The trees were free for the taking, and a family might spend an entire day in the mountains selecting the "perfect tree." The prize would then be carefully cut and hauled off through the snowy forest by a sled or lashed to the saddle of a horse. All varieties of conifers were used, but early accounts indicate that where abundant, the thick-branched and beautiful Colorado Blue Spruce was the most treasured of all Christmas trees.

However, during the early years before the turn of the century, the vast majority of Great Plains homesteaders living far from the mountains spent the holidays without Christmas trees. Occasionally, a sod house family might cut a bare cottonwood along the bank of a prairie stream and cover its branches with cotton batting. The sparse deciduous trees in no way, however, tempered the desire to obtain an evergreen if and when they became available through private entrepreneurs, who shipped them to the prairie communities on the railroads beginning in the late 1890s. After the passage of the Timber Culture Act in 1873, which encouraged the planting of greenbelts across the plains, a hardy cedar tree or cedar bush might bring some greenery inside to grace the simple homes of plains farmers or isolated ranchers.

Indeed, the determination of homesteaders to celebrate the Yuletide is revealed in the adaptations and innovations they devised on the treeless prairie. In numerous cases, dried tumbleweeds, sagebrush, or even pieces of scrap wood nailed together were decorated at Christmastime. Homesteaders on the sod house frontier would go to extreme lengths to simulate the beloved Christmas tree for their children.

The custom of having Christmas trees was generally more widespread among the residents of mining towns situated within the mountains of the Rocky Mountain West. Not only did large, stately evergreens adorn the parlors of gothic houses but mining town churches and business establishments as well benefited from the community's proximity to the forest when the time arrived to decorate for the holidays. In 1878 the Georgetown, Colorado, newspaper, the *Miner,* reported on trimmings inside that town's Grace Episcopal Church.

> The church was very handsomely decorated with evergreens, wreathes [sic], etc., and the gigantic Christmas tree in the background predicated happiness for the little ones, which was fully the case, there being an estimated 200 children present.

Saloons, dance halls, and gambling parlors in the mountains also decorated their interiors with Christmas trees. The fragrant conifers would be profusely loaded with paper cutouts, strings of popcorn, liquor labels, bottle caps, and in more than one instance, fried oysters. The eclectically decorated pines appeared to blend quite naturally with the gaudy and cluttered trappings of the cosmopolitan mining towns.

For city dwellers living near the Rockies, it was customary for families, and sometimes entire neighborhoods, to venture into the mountains for the day or even overnight to find Christmas trees. The day would be spent searching for spruce or balsam, followed by a rollicking picnic in the snow if the weather permitted. Toward the turn of the century, enterprising individuals would travel into the hills before Christmas and, unrestricted by legal sanctions, cut fresh trees for commercial sale back in the city. On December 22, 1900, the *Denver Times* reported on Christmas trees for sale along Denver's upper Sixteenth Street.

> At the upper end of the shopping district where the carriage trade mostly finds its way, rows of Christmas trees fresh from their mountain homes lean over a fence, appealing directly to passersby. Across the street are windows filled with the choicest things that money can bring from the uttermost parts of the earth; things of beauty and a joy for cultivated tastes.

During the early years, city dwellers, like their rural counterparts, made their own Christmas ornaments from cardboard, bright paper, cotton, and other household items. Strings of popcorn and cranberries were always popular throughout the nineteenth century. Victorian ornaments made commercially of tin, cardboard, and wax, depicting animals, St. Nicholas figures, children, and angels were a rare commodity on the frontier before the 1880s. With the development of the blown glass ornament by 1890, however, Christmas tree decorations were revolutionized. Perfected through the use of lead molds by German glassblowers in the town of Lauscha, north of Nuremberg, the intricate ornaments imitating birds, dogs, bears, cottages, musical instruments, cherubs, and numerous other figures were imported by the millions to the United States by novelty magnate F. W. Woolworth. The glass ornaments, which were relatively inexpensive, found their way west to early department and general stores throughout the Rocky Mountains, beginning in the 1890s, to grace the luxuriant Victorian Christmas trees of a Walter von Richthofen or a Molly Brown.

Before the invention of electric lighting, Christmas trees were gracefully illuminated with small wax candles. Tin candle holders were clipped to the delicate limbs of the Christmas tree and counterweighted by small lead balls attached to the candle holders by short strings. Lighting candles so close to dry branches was dangerous, and numerous newspaper accounts from the nineteenth century reported a family's Christmas ruined when the tree caught fire, devastating a room or, occasionally, an entire house. Many a family Santa Claus became so involved with distributing gifts that he did not notice that the cotton fringes of his homemade suit were blazing gloriously up his back. Although insurance underwriters discouraged the use of candles on Christmas trees, the dangerous custom continued to be an integral part of the Christmas celebration and was practiced with regularity for the first decade or so of the twentieth century.

Ordinarily the tree would be secretly delivered to the house a week or so before Christmas and decorated by Mother and Father late on Christmas Eve. Early on Christmas morning, the family would gather around the tree, and the candles would be ceremoniously lighted—several handy buckets of water were placed in the room in case of the unthinkable. After a short time, the candles were extinguished and the family would settle down to open their presents.

With the Edison patent of the incandescent light bulb in 1879, Christmas tree decorations were once again revolutionized. Within three years after the invention, the world's first electrically lighted Christmas tree was displayed at the New York City home of Edward Johnson, a close colleague of Thomas Edison. By the very next Christmas season, the innovation had reached the base of the Rocky Mountains. On December 26, 1883, the *Rocky Mountain News* reported on formalities associated with the first known electric lighting of a Christmas tree in Denver or the Rocky

Mountain West. The tree was located inside the sanctuary of the Lawrence Street Methodist Church.

> The exercises opened promptly at 7:30 p.m. The Church was beautifully decorated and in the center of the platform stood the lovely Christmas tree lighted by thirty electric globes which gleamed with a daylight brightness from the boughs. The electric display was under the direction of Prof. Short, and was a great success. It is the first time a Christmas tree in Denver has ever been lighted by electricity, and, beyond an occasional flickering, the illumination worked admirably and without accident. The trees were trimmed with popcorn, gold and silver lace and red balls. Around the room were some fine decorations including a bell, a star, etc., designed and executed by Miss Gale Hall. The other decorations were arranged by the various young ladies of the (Sunday) school. The electric lights were provided by Messrs. Haynes and Suchrist.

Decorating Christmas trees with glass balls and strings of electric lights continues today, mostly unchanged from the late years of the nineteenth century. The custom even extends to adorning evergreens and other shrubbery outdoors. In fact, a man from Denver by the name of David Dwight Sturgeon is generally credited with originating outdoor Christmas lighting. An electrician by trade, Sturgeon sought a way to bring some Christmas cheer to his ten-year-old son, who lay dying of a fatal illness in the family home during the Yuletide season of 1914. Dipping some ordinary light bulbs in red and green paint, Sturgeon strung the colorful lights on some pine trees located outside the boy's window. The newspapers reported on the outdoor display, and soon buggies and horseless carriages began driving past the street to see the novelty. As the custom spread, the city of Denver even sponsored contests, beginning in 1918, complete with prizes awarded to neighborhoods with the most elaborate displays of outdoor Christmas lights. The Sturgeon boy lived for seven more years and witnessed what became a widespread tradition throughout the United States.

Although most commercially grown trees for sale today in the Rocky Mountain region originate on "farms" in the Pacific Northwest or the Great Lakes states, modern westerners who wish to savor the traditions of their ancestors by obtaining a native evergreen can do so. With the establishment of the U.S. Bureau of Forestry during the early years of the twentieth century, the vast timberlands of the West came under the protection of the federal government. The modern resident of the Rocky Mountain West may still cut a Christmas tree in accordance with certain regulations. In areas where young trees need to be thinned to keep the forests healthy, citizens can obtain permits from the Forest Service to harvest a tree in designated areas. For the two or three weekends before Christmas, the modern celebrants can be seen trudging up snowy back roads in the mountains, ax or saw in hand, continuing a much-cherished and nostalgic legacy from our pioneer past.

· Nineteen ·

Gifts
1804–1900

Ever since the beginning of American expansion into the vast stronghold of the Rocky Mountain empire, Christmas giving has been tradition. Even while fighting against nature for their very survival, the early explorers of the western regions of the Louisiana Territory took time out to share rations of whiskey with their comrades on Christmas Day. Once the mountain men established semipermanent residence in the region, Christmas became a time for exchanging gifts of food and clothing with the Native American inhabitants. Seated around a smoldering log fire inside a buffalo hide tepee, the trapper and the Indian would share a smoke, exchange trinkets and buckskin clothing, and keep Christmas.

In the northern Rockies of Montana and Idaho, the French Canadian fur trappers further formalized the custom in the ceremony of *feu de joie,* in which people of both races would seat themselves inside a circle of bonfires to exchange gifts. From the earliest days of Salt Lake City during the late 1840s, the Mormons exchanged homemade presents at Christmas. In numerous upstart mining camps dotting the raw frontier, early prospectors would pause during the Yuletide to share a drink or a pouch of tobacco with friends and strangers alike.

As legions of pioneer farmers swept across the barren prairies leading toward the mantle of the Rocky Mountains, families with children appeared in the West in large numbers for the first time. Within the dark interiors of the musty-smelling dugouts and sod houses situated on the unbroken horizon of the Great Plains, the child's Christmas became rooted in the traditions of the far West. Toys were of course scarce on the isolated farming frontier, and adaptation and improvisation in this as well as all aspects of daily living was taken for granted. After long days in the field, Father would spend hours by the light of an "old hussy" oil lamp whittling toy cannons or horses from scraps of wood for his sons. Mother, too, sacrificed precious time to ensure her daughter would have a merry Christmas. Through cold dark hours, while their children were fast asleep, homesteading parents would fashion simple homemade gifts: dresses for dolls were sewn together from scraps of worn-out garments; dolls with wooden bodies and papier-mâché heads were expertly molded; wooden rattles and rocking horses, carved and patiently hand painted, were the only Christmas presents frontier youngsters might receive.

If a railroad was nearby, there might be the anticipation of receiving a "parcel" from relatives back East, but with unreliable mails and train schedules and uncertain weather, many a Christmas Day passed on the prairies without the long-anticipated package from the folks "back home." After the popularization of Santa Claus among Union armies during the Civil War, stockings were hung on bedposts, walls, and in other convenient places. Filled with baked confections, small dolls fashioned from potatoes, and, if the family was fortunate enough, stick cinnamon, apples, and peppermints, the bulging socks were a joyful sight to small children of the sod house frontier. Mrs. W. S. Carpenter of Horse Creek, Wyoming, recalled treats of candy and fresh fruit hauled thirty miles from Cheyenne by wagon as constituting the only Christmas presents she might receive during lean years.

By the 1880s, the Montgomery Ward catalog became the basic mode of Christmas shopping for farm and ranch families. Children would spend hours in the early fall pondering over new dresses, dolls, toy guns, and drums. Orders would be mailed months in advance, and when packages arrived at the nearest town by railroad, the buckboard would be hitched up for the long journey across the rough prairie to the depot.

Itinerant peddlers who roamed the plains and foothills were another source of supply for Christmas gifts. These salesmen traveling on horseback or buckboard would bring fabric, buttons, thread, trimmings, and trinkets that could be purchased on the spot. Mrs. Donald Clark of Cheyenne remembers purchasing sewing materials during the summer months from these traveling salesmen to be used for making Christmas gifts in the fall.

> Long before Christmas and helped by one or two of the younger girls (we) would get busy on the sewing. Dresses, petticoats, and doll clothes were made for the girls, shirts and underwear for the boys. And, of course, there were mittens, stockings and scarves to be knitted for everyone.

With the coming of the railroad, Denver became the principal commercial center of the Rocky Mountain West. During the years following 1870, the metropolis was connected to the booming mining towns in the mountains by a growing network of freight roads and rails. Subsequently, the Queen City attracted a host of merchants, including the determined pioneer dry goods retailer and tradesmen J. C. Penney, who provided Rocky Mountain residents with material goods. From lavish department stores downtown, the middle class of the Rocky Mountains, throughout the later years of the nineteenth century, loaded their wagons with goods fresh from the East to make their lives more enjoyable. Local merchants in the mining towns of the interior ordered merchandise from these stores or from the East and had it shipped over snow-covered mountain passes by narrow-gauge railroad.

Christmas shopping for the urban dweller was of course much more convenient than for secluded homesteaders and ranchers. A Saturday before Christmas during the last two decades of the nineteenth century might find a proper Victorian family leaving their fashionable home on Capitol Hill to board a cable car or, by the 1890s, an electric trolley operating along Denver's Fifteenth Street (the second-oldest electric street railway in the world). After lunch at the Windsor Hotel or the Brown Palace, the family would join crowds of people prowling the shopping district along Sixteenth Street. Clad in a tweed suit and derby hat, Father might hold the hand of a small daughter properly bundled in a velvet coat and cap. The atmosphere would be electric as the family turned onto Sixteenth Street and saw the throngs of excited holiday buyers. Near the turn of the century, the *Denver Times* described the following scene:

Sixteenth street is nowadays a much traveled thoroughfare. Not but that there are other streets—but this one is like the famous corner in New York [Broadway and Twenty-third].

So it is with Sixteenth street. Some time during the fortnight before Christmas every man, woman and child in Denver who believes in Santa Claus makes from one to a dozen pilgrimages between Tremont and Larimer, on Sixteenth.

From store to store go patient mothers marshaling the eager youngsters shouting unlimited wants amidst abounding bright decorations, heaps upon heaps of wondrous toys and mountains of multi-colored sweets.

Sweethearts trudge up one side of the street and down the other, arm in arm, casually looking in at this window and then at that, breathlessly noting likes and dislikes in order to slip down alone the next day and make their momentous purchases. The surging throngs will go the rounds, adding parcel after parcel to already cumbersome loads, vowing and declaring in the same old way that another year will find them through with shopping fully a month ahead so that Christmas week will not catch them belated on Sixteenth street.

Filtering into the crowd, the family might pass a sign for the Denver Packing Company advertising "Oysters, Fish, Game and Poultry for Christmas." If the year was 1889, Father might notice as he passed Sixteenth and Curtis that Sophie Eyre was playing the Tabor Grand Opera House. Soon the family would encounter a host of department stores to entice the anxious children. Entering the venerable firm of Daniels and Fisher, the children would notice the abundance of mechanical toys, steam trains, iron toys, musical instruments, and rows of porcelain dolls. A sign reads, "The Basement is Santa Claus headquarters in Denver—Specials on bicycles and high wheelers."

Around the corner at Fifteenth and Larimer, the May Company advertised "Men's Suits and Overcoats, $10, and $20—Holiday Headgear, Genuine Sealskin Caps worth $15 each—Brighton, Windsor and Polo shapes, only 3 dozen left—take your choice for $7.00." For women there were "gold tipped umbrellas $1.65—real value $3.00," silk blouses, and fur muffs. Silk and cashmere scarves sold for $10, and there was a special on women's hosiery—"a complete line from Allen, Sally & Co., London England including fast black—3 pair for fifty cents." A huge banner over the women's department boasted, "You'll never again meet with the values we are offering you!"

Joslins and the Denver Dry Goods Company suggested for men "slippers, smoking jackets, morning jackets and pure silk night robes in the $15 price range, toilet sets, starched collars and cuffs for under $2; Holiday Presents from Five Cents to Five Hundred Dollars—Open Evenings until Christmas."

The end of the day would surely find the parcel-laden family visiting Monash's "Christmas Fair—The People's Toy Store" on the corner of Sixteenth and Champa. The huge "bargain basement" was selling "sleds and coasters for $1.65, Shoofly Rocking Horses—forty-eight cents to sixty-five cents, the largest selection of dolls in the city for under $1"and "boys' velocipedes [tricycles] $1.35–$1.95." Naturally there were Christmas tree decorations for sale at the fair—"12 tin candle holders" sold for a nickel.

By evening, as the sun dipped over the distant peaks of the front range, the bone-weary family would make its way back home, burdened with too many packages and fully aware that with the dawn of a new century rapidly approaching, the commercialization of Christmas had come to the Rocky Mountain West.

Epilogue

I
n these modern times as we gather with family and friends around the Christmas hearth, we may speculate nostalgically about the Yuletide practices from our pioneer past. And like our forefathers of generations gone by, we continue to innovate and adapt old traditions to the resources and technology of the present. Although we might continue to venture into the mountains each Yuletide season to carefully select and cut our Christmas tree, we nevertheless enjoy all the benefits of modern invention and convenience in decorating and illuminating this most widespread of American Christmas traditions. The newest strand of colored, twinkling lights might shine brightly next to an old Victorian glass ornament that has been passed down through the generations as a loved and treasured heirloom. Strings of "snowy popcorn and cran-berries" may still adorn our trees, as they did in the world Rose Georgina Kingsley knew. The seasonal carols we sing may be long-enduring family traditions, and the mouth-watering delicacies on our Christmas tables, although prepared with the most modern conveniences, may be old regional or family recipes.

Throughout the Rocky Mountain West, and indeed across the entire nation, the origins of community celebrations and customs can be traced far into the past. Palmer Lake, Colorado, is but one example of a regional community that has revived the old northern European tradition of the annual Yule log hunt, first brought to the West during the mining rushes of the nineteenth century. In rural communities throughout the former frontier, American Legion posts and other civic organizations still sponsor the venerable turkey shoot, using the modern innovations of trap or skeet. In the Southwest, the Indians still dance, blending ancient custom with modern Christian practice. These midnight rituals continue to be acted out in the isolated pueblos, seemingly unchanged from a century ago. Urban festivals at Christmastime annually depict a rich heritage from the eras of our ancestors.

But the most cherished memories remain those connected with the home; in the bosom of the family unit, loved ones and their family's practices from Christmases long past are fondly remembered every December 25. "The best of the old and the best of the new" most appropriately defines the family Christmas today, as it did one hundred years ago. After all, that is the way it should be.

Bibliography

Manuscripts

Larimer, William. Papers. Colorado Historical Society, Denver, Colorado.

Periodical Articles and Publications of Learned Societies

Collins, Catharine Wever. "Letters of Catharine Wever Collins, 1863–1864. *Colorado Magazine* 31, no. 4 (October 1954): 251–55.

"Editor's Notes." *Colorado Magazine* 45, no. 3 (Winter 1968): 247.

Hronek, Sheri. "Pioneer Christmas." *Nebraskaland* 43, no. 12 (December 1965): 8–11.

Love, Louise. "Christmas on Early-Day Wyoming Ranches." *Cow Country* (December 1953): 5, 24.

McGavin, Cecil E. "How the Pioneers Celebrated Christmas." *Improvement Era Magazine* 4, no. 12 (December 1941): 724, 743.

Monnett, John H. "Good Neighbors." *Western Horseman* 56, no. 12 (December 1991): 10–11.

Peterson, Walter F., ed. "Christmas on the Plains: Elizabeth Bacon Custer's Nostalgic Memories of Holiday Seasons on the Frontier." *American West* 1, no. 4 (Fall 1964): 53–57.

Pillsbury, Dorthy. "Enchanted Christmas." *New Mexico Magazine* 26, no. 12 (December 1948): 19, 46–48.

———. "Pom Poms at Christmas." *Desert Magazine* 13, no. 2 (December 1949): 18–20.

Rice, Cyrus R. "Experiences of a Pioneer Missionary." *Collections of the Kansas State Historical Society* 13 (1913–1914): 298–305.

Spencer, Frank. "The Fremont Expedition of 1848." *Colorado Magazine,* July 1929: 141–144.

Stone, Arthur L. "Christmas in Montana, 1813." *Montana: Magazine of Western History* 6, no. 1 (January 1965): 1–8.

Thomas, D. G. "How Rock Springs Celebrated Christmas in '78." *Annals of Wyoming* 27, no. 1 (April 1955): 31–34.

Waddy, O. L. "Christmas on the Plains." *Western Horseman* 18, no. 12 (December 1953): 28–29.

Young, Eleanor. "St. Nick and the Early Colorado Gold Camps: An Account of the Early Beginning of the Great City of Denver." *Montana: Magazine of Western History* 9, no. 1 (Winter 1959): 20–25.

Newspapers

Denver Field and Farm. December 16, 1895; December 23, 1911.

Denver Post. December 27, 1892.

Denver Times. December 27, 1891; December 26, 1892; December 22, 1898.

Georgetown Miner. December 26, 1898.

Rocky Mountain News. December 26, 1883; December 25, 1889; December 23, 1984.

Books

Adams, Andy. *The Log of a Cowboy.* Lincoln: University of Nebraska Press, 1964.

Arps, Louise Ward. *Denver in Slices.* Athens, Ohio: Swallow Press, 1983.

Atherton, Lewis. *The Cattle Kings.* Bloomington: Indiana University Press, 1961.

Baur, John E. *Christmas on the American Frontier.* Caldwell, Idaho: Caxton Publishing Co., 1959.

Bickerstaff, Laura M. *Pioneer Artists of Taos.* Rev. ed. Denver: Old West Publishing Co., 1983.

Billington, Ray Allen, and Martin Ridge. *Westward Expansion: A History of the American Frontier.* 5th ed. New York: Macmillan Co., 1982.

Brady, Cyrus Townsend. *Recollections of a Missionary in the Great West.* New York: Charles Scribner's Sons, 1900.

Dale, Edward E. *The Range Cattle Industry.* Norman: University of Oklahoma Press, 1930.

Dallas, Sandra. *Colorado Ghost Towns and Mining Camps.* Norman: University of Oklahoma Press, 1985.

———. *Gaslight and Gingerbread.* Athens, Ohio: Swallow Press, 1984.

Dorsett, Lyle, and Michael McCarthy. *The Queen City: A History of Denver.* 2d ed. Pruett Publishing Co., 1986.

Dyer, Alvin E., ed. *The Cattle Queen of Montana.* Spokane: Dyer Press, 1901.

Ebbutt, Percy. *Emigrant Life in Kansas.* London: Swan Sonnenschein & Co., 1886.

Goodykoontz, Colin B. *Colorado: Short Studies of Its Past and Present.* Boulder: University of Colorado Press, 1927.

Hooker, William Francis. *The Bullwhacker: Adventures of a Frontier Freighter*. New York: World Book Co., 1924.

House, Ernest. *A Life Worth Living*. Pasadena: Trails End Publishing Co., 1948.

Jackson, Donald, ed. *Journals of Zebulon Montgomery Pike: With Letters and Related Documents*. Norman: University of Oklahoma Press, 1966.

Kingsley, Charles, ed. *South by West, or Winter in the Rocky Mountains and Spring in Mexico*. London: W. Ibsiter & Co., 1874.

Kohl, Edith Eudora. *Denver's First Christmas*. Denver: A. B. Hirschfeld Press, 1944.

Noel, Thomas J. *Richthofen's Montclair: A Pioneer Denver Suburb*. Boulder: Pruett Publishing Co., 1976.

Quaife, Milton, ed. *Kit Carson's Autobiography*. Lincoln: University of Nebraska Press, 1967.

Remington, Frederic. *Pony Tracks*. Norman: University of Oklahoma Press, 1961.

Sansom, William. *A Book of Christmas*. New York: McGraw-Hill Co., 1968.

Smith, Phyllis. *A Look at Boulder: From Settlement to City*. Boulder: Pruett Publishing Co., 1981.

Snyder, Phillip V. *The Christmas Tree Book*. New York: Viking Press, 1976.

Taylor, George R., ed. *The Turner Thesis Concerning the Role of the Frontier in American History*. 3d ed. Lexington, Mass.: D. C. Heath and Co., 1972.

Taylor, Lewis, and Joanne Young. *Christmas in the Southwest*. New York: Holt, Rinehart and Winston, 1973.

Thwaites, Reuben G., ed. *Original Journals of the Lewis and Clark Expedition, 1804–1806*. 8 vols. New York: Putnam and Sons, 1904.

Utley, Robert M. *The Last Days of the Sioux Nation*. New Haven: Yale University Press, 1963.

Index